WICKEDLY SMART WOMEN

*Trusting Intuition, Taking
Action, Transforming Worlds*

To Suzanette,
May your dream
become an enormous
reality

WICKEDLY SMART WOMEN

Trusting Intuition, Taking Action, Transforming Worlds

Anjel B Hartwell

Action Takers Publishing™
San Diego, California

Action Takers Publishing™

www.actiontakerspublishing.com

Paperback ISBN: 978-1-956665-22-2

ebook ISBN: 978-1-956665-23-9

Cover Design by Sam Art Studio

Printed in the United States of America

Table of Contents

Introduction

What a magical time we live in. There's been a rising tide of women all over the world that have been awakened to their own power. The power that lives within. They have begun to listen to that still, small voice inside. To trust their own knowing. To believe that what they are feeling, seeing in their dreams, and hearing whispered from their heart of hearts is valid, true, beautiful and worthy.

What's even more beautiful, though? Beyond trusting their intuition, these women are mustering up the courage and taking bold, decisive, sometimes even radical action to energize their dreams and visions. To materialize what they see in their inner world and to bring it forth into the material world.

As a result, worlds are being transformed! The world of business, the world of healthcare, the world of art, the world of entertainment, the world of finance, and so many more worlds within worlds are being rapidly and radically changed across the planet, in all cultures, all societies, all fields of endeavor you will find these women – shamelessly and vibrantly leading the way, expressing and embodying the new archetype of the Wickedly Smart Woman. She who remembers her own power. She who engages in the collaborative co-creation of the more beautiful world that is seen in her imagination and held within her heart. She who is standing fully in her self-trust and speaking out to serve her purpose.

In the pages of this book, dear reader, you will find the incredible stories of just a small segment of the much larger and globally emerging group of Wickedly Smart Women who are role modeling what is possible and oftentimes bringing into reality what many may have believed to be impossible. Despite the challenges, despite social and cultural conditioning that has been strapping women down for millennia, despite the blowback that liberation of these feminine forces of nature have had to face, here they are in all their beautiful glory, here to inspire you with their SHEROIC stories.

We are so grateful that you chose to invest in getting to know these wonderful women. We want you to know that if you have this book in your hands then it's guaranteed that you are also a member of the growing sisterhood of Wickedly Smart Women. We encourage you to find the reinforcement and affirmation in the words of these women so that you feel empowered to be bold and shine your radiant light, too!

We welcome you with open arms, open hearts, and encourage you to find the inspiration here to take your own stand, share your own story, and provide whatever support you can to your sisters in spirit wherever you are in the world. Humanity and the planet are in the changing times now and we invite you to join us while you Trust Your Intuition, Take Action & Transform Worlds!

A Special Note About the Charity

Building a Playmaker Movement

1 in 3 kids experience some form of life-threatening adversity like homelessness, abuse, or community violence. Research shows that a positive relationship with just one caring adult in early childhood can change that child's life entirely.

The Playmaker Project puts optimism into practice, providing training and support for a growing network of more than 16,000 professionals who create positive relationships and joy-filled environments that children need to heal, learn and thrive. We call them Playmakers.

100% of the net proceeds from the sales of this book is being donated to the Life is Good Playmakers Foundation. Visit them at www.LifeIsGood.com.

CHAPTER 1

Change Your Name – Change Your Life!

Anjel B Hartwell

Dare to be BOLD – never mind BOLD – dare to be YOU – the YOU that you really are – deep underneath all the labels that were put on you by family conditioning, by culture, by society, by educators, by religion – because underneath ALL of that – there is someone – someone who came here to be BOLD, BEAUTIFUL, and BRAZEN and that is YOU!

I remember when....

I was the dutiful daughter of the alcoholic dad and the co-dependent borderline personality disordered mom. I was the one that got all the A's because, well, that's what good girls do, isn't it? I was at the top of my class when I graduated – 27 out of 123 students – oh and that was a year EARLY? Yep, I skipped senior year all together and went right on to college as a National Merit Scholarship Qualifying Test (NMSQT) commended scholar.

I wore the clothes that my mom bought for me (looked like a fashion model from the 1950s) and that didn't go over really well in the '70s and early '80s when I was growing up and getting ready to take on the world.

I did a little college because that was what was expected of me – I had the grades, after all, and had been prepped for it for years. There was one small problem, though: two weeks before graduating high school, my dad lost his job. I don't know exactly why, but I'm quite sure that the drinking had a lot to do with it and of course my mom's story skewed in his favor and against the owners of the company. It was their fault. They didn't appreciate him and all his years of service. So we only had enough to pay for that first year at Penn State. After that, I was on my own.

But not really, because I carried with me all the stories, all the myths, all the labels, and all the expectations of what it meant to be a woman and what it meant to be a contributing member of what we term as "society." I left college and went to work. There was no money for me for year two. Dad was busy drowning his sorrows while mom was trying to put together and operate HIS business.

Time went by and I ended up getting my own house and my own dysfunctional husband – chose to marry him because the "clock" (as the world says) was ticking and I KNEW I needed to hurry up and get married even if I didn't share the same values as he did because it was TIME I was supposed to have a baby! I did the role playing really well. I even had all his pants lined up by color, all his shirts ironed, hot food on the table every night, and not a peep out of me when he'd spend every spare minute of his time up at his parent's house gambling and playing cards till the wee hours of the morning. Maybe after the BABY things would work out better or at least the way I was always led to believe they would.

NOT.

Several years and a LOT of drama and trauma later, I WOKE UP! OMG! I'll never forget when I finally gave myself permission to want what I wanted, to find out what excited and interested ME, and to actually ACT on some of those desires (even the ones that seemed more than a little bit kooky and out there). My first DARING act of BOLDNESS was to tell my husband I wanted a DIVORCE. I declared my independence on September 9, 2001. There was something in the air as we moved through that fateful fall – an awakening time for more than just me. I know it now, but in those moments all I knew was that MY OWN world was coming apart all around me. The rest of the country? Well, I prayed for those people, but I really spent most of the time praying for myself.

I shut out the outside world pretty quickly. After all, it was truly crazy and didn't seem to be working real well in spite of all the "rules and regs" about how to be, act, do life. I went in. What I found there was nothing short of MIRACULOUS. I started a healing journey, a journey to discover the me under all the roles. I spent most of the year of my divorce just waiting, but after the waiting was over, I really started to break loose in a big way. Right after the marriage ended I went into my office. At the time, I was a real estate developer and consultant at the tail end of building and selling out an award winning multi-million dollar development of 51 single family houses, 56 apartments and an office building. I had also just wrapped up the end of my term as the National Chairperson for my trade association. I played that role really well, too, talking to senators on Capitol Hill, being interviewed by the Wall Street Journal, NY Times, Washington Post (all the biggies). I was at the TOP of that game playing by all the rules and on the outside was a "winner."

I walked into the office in December of '02 and, DARING ACT OF BOLDNESS 2, I told my business partner I was all done. He asked me what I was going to do and DARE I SAY IT??? Out of my mouth quite literally FELL the words "I'm going to be a crystal healer." As you might expect, he looked at me like I had 3 heads! The funny thing about that is that I'd never even had a crystal healing before. I had been reading about crystals in my spare time and had begun making jewelry high-lighting the healing qualities of the stones. I'd even started taking some of the pieces out of my "Studio space" (the little desk off on one side of my bedroom) and 18 different local shops had my work available for sale.

My next and probably most transformative DARING ACT OF BOLDNESS was in discovering and then CLAIMING (including le-gally) my FIRST Spiritually delivered "true name." There's a story that goes with that. In January of '03 I was on my massage therapist's table, Sandy. She was REALLY great at massage therapy. I remember lying there on her table thinking to myself, "This woman was MADE to do this. What was I made to do? Who Am I?" Well, that question all by itself OPENED THE CHANNEL.

In one of my very first experiences of clairaudience I received clear-ly in my ear the words: "You are a WILDFIRE." I was contemplating the action of becoming a healer and really feeling confused about how I was going to put myself out there. I mean, what are the RESULTS of "Crystal Healing" for God's Sake? When I heard those words, though, I got it. I knew what it meant. My work is to be like a wildfire, a hot, blazing, wild, incredible force that transforms everything in its path. Did you know that there are some seeds that lie dormant on the forest floor for 100 years and can only be germinated by the intense heat of a wildfire?

It took about another year and a half almost (a year and a half of studying metaphysics including crystals, reiki, Shamballa Multidimen-sional Healing, and becoming initiated as a medicine carrier in the shamanic traditions of the Inka of the high Andes)– before I received my first name. It was a beautiful May morning, the morning after the VERY FIRST teaching I offered in a small local shop about crystals and crystal healing.

I woke up that morning and sat down to my morning routine of yoga and meditation – this morning was a bit different, though. I was holding in my hand a piece of black tourmaline – given to me the night before by the shop owner. I wasn't "searching" to be renamed, by the way; I was only doing my morning routine. I was opening to Spirit and allowing myself to receive whatever grace had to offer me that day. I sat in silence with the crystal and suddenly there in my mind's eye appeared the Master Jeshua (Jesus to some), beside him on the right was Master Germaine (of the Violet Flame), and on the left was Archangel Michael. As I sat there in rapturous wonder, Master Jeshua laid his hands on my head and said quite clearly to me, "You are Amethyst." "Yes," I thought to myself, exactly. In that moment, too, I "knew" I was A. Wyldfyre (the A had come a year and a half before) and now both names came together. Amethyst Wyldfyre – Yes! This name came from the heavens to me. It was up to me to receive it and make it real. Legally.

A dozen years passed after Amethyst Wyldfyre arrived on the scene. During that time, an international reputation was built as a speaker, author, and healer helping women to feel great speaking and powerful asking for money. Amethyst (I) made multiple millions from home, mostly in pajamas or yoga pants while raising a son through adolescence, using the phone and fierce faith to be heard by millions and to serve a global audience. She was part of the rising tide of women who rose up to be seen, heard, and hired in the first two decades of the new millennium.

Spring of 2016, and another life-changing rite of passage occurred, once again involving addiction, domestic violence, and abuse issues. This time was with my son who was named after my father. DARING ACT OF BOLDNESS - It was time for me to die to the role of mother and for Amethyst Wyldfyre to die, too. Master Jesus came and off she went with him in the early hours of May 1 after a harrowing night of being trapped in the basement told I'd be cut up into little pieces and thrown in the river by the child I bore who was high on benzos and fentanyl and had been on a 3-day bender that came to its ugly head that night.

I managed to escape through the grace of TRUSTING my intuition and a brief moment in time when he went upstairs to pee. I "HEARD" loudly, "GO NOW" and managed to get out of the bulkhead upon which a large, heavy garden pot had been placed to prevent my escape. I ran for the forest (thankfully I had my phone) and, gasping for breath leaning at the base of a giant pine, called his father who immediately began yelling at me. Another AWAKENING MOMENT when I realized that who I'd called for help WASN'T helping. Hung up, called the police and OFFICER FRIEND (you can't make this shit up – that's seriously what his last name was!) came to pick me up and bring me to the station where a report was filed as an arrest was being made.

The next day I heard a still small voice. This time bubbling UP from the inside. It said: "You are Emerald now." Emerald Peaceful GreenForest. WHAT?? Ok...within three days I was at the courthouse, filed the papers, and changed my name again.

Four years later (2020), after a long and difficult road of attempting to recover my mental well-being, having my business and income drop precipitously close to bankruptcy, rebranding and launching my first and then my second podcast I had another "knowing" that it was time to seek help to bring to closure any remaining open wounds from that night in the basement. I sought out a former therapist for support. One of the many things I mentioned during the intake was that my money situation had spiraled out of control in a downward direction in addition to my health (mental and physical) since that night in the basement. She was one of my early teachers on the spiritual path in addition to being my therapist for a while. She also listened to her intuition and one of the first things she asked was, "did you get the numerology done on the name Emerald Peaceful GreenForest?" No....no, I did not.

I left her office that day and followed her intuitive suggestion to find out what I could about my name. I discovered the Kabalarian Philosophy, had my name analysis done and wouldn't you know.... Emerald Peaceful GreenForest was bad for EVERYTHING for me!! Health, No Good; Relationships, No Good; Money and Business, No Good! I immediately invested in the balanced name recommendation service and got back a list of 120 first names, 120 last names, and 120 middle names starting with one of three letters. Anjel B Hartwell was selected by me! Within a week, my name was changed legally AGAIN and within 10 days I had my first $25K client in four years enroll to work with me and my business has continued to recover along with my health and my relationships. I changed my name a third time and have been on the upward spiral ever since!

Sometimes change can feel daunting. And changing your name (especially when you've not once but twice built a business reputation and brand) is not just bold and daring, but some might even consider it slightly insane!

I'm here now, though, on the other side of the drama, living and loving my Wealthy Life By Design™ and a testament to Trusting Intuition, Taking Action & Transforming Worlds – starting with my own. Blessedly, my son is now healthy and liberated from the addictions and our relationship has reconciled, too.

Creating change is a process of engaging your conscious awareness.

These are my 7 C's For Creating Conscious Change:

1. Clarity – Know what you want
2. Courage – Find the HEART to go after it
3. Consult – Invest in support from magical mentors, coaches, consultants to advise you
4. Create – Take the leap and engage in Inspired Action

5. Check In – Assess and adjust to align with what you REALLY want

6. Choose – Accept and Allow yourself permission to reach your dreams

7. Celebrate – Enjoy what manifests from your devotion to creating your Wealthy Life By Design™

The start of my transformational journey 21 years ago was precipitated by the question, "What Do YOU Want?" It was asked by someone who'd known me since I was six and was the first time I'd ever been asked that directly. In fact, when she asked, it came as something of a shock that I could even HAVE wants of my own. People-pleasing and conforming to community and cultural standards was so ingrained that just the question perturbed my psyche enough to get me moving on the path to where I am today. So I'll close by giving YOU that question to ponder, too….

What is it that YOU Want?

What is coming to you – that you need only OPEN to in order to receive. Who are you really? Dare to be BOLD. There is only ONE you – ever. Be who you were meant to be. Create Conscious Change Fearlessly.

ANJEL B HARTWELL

Anjel B Hartwell (FKA Emerald Peaceful GreenForest FKA Amethyst Wyldfyre) is an internationally known Speaker, Spiritual Leader, and Transformation Artist. An 8X Award Winning #1 Internationally Ranked Podcast Host & Executive Producer and Founding Visionary of Creative Age Consulting Group, she is hired by leading visionary entrepreneurs and global change agents who want to become massively magnetic to money so that they can fund their movements and fulfill their missions.

Find out more about Anjel at www.wickedlysmartwomen.com.

CHAPTER 2

Faith. Erases. Anxious. Reactions.

Lynda Sunshine West

"When your fear is strong, your faith is weak. When your faith is strong, your fear is weak. Tap into your faith and do it BECAUSE you're scared." ~Lynda Sunshine West

It was a day like any other, so I thought.

I woke up with nothing important on my mind and hadn't even considered what the new year would bring. I used to set New Year's Resolutions, but never followed through on any of them, so I stopped setting them when I was about thirty years old. Who was it that decided we needed to start new on the first day of the year? What kind of craziness is that, right?

Every year on January 1st you decide that you're going to make a huge shift in your life. Some of the most common resolutions are to stop smoking, stop drinking, stop gambling, start exercising, start eating healthy, start saving for retirement. You start off gung-ho and, by about January 15 (if you're lucky that you made it fifteen days), you've failed.

This may not be your experience, but this was mine: Every friggin' year. 1) set a resolution to change my life, 2) do great for a few days,

3) start falling off the wagon, 4) break the resolution, and 5) feel like a failure. Repeat cycle next year. As I think back on that time, I was just setting a New Year's Resolution because that was what everyone around me did. Monkey see, monkey do.

But this day was different. Something snapped inside of me. My intuition was firing on all cylinders. God spoke to me loud and clear.

It was the morning of January 1, 2015. I woke up and heard someone yelling… in my head. It was me yelling at myself, "I have so many fears. They're stopping me from living my life. I'm going to break through one fear a day this year. Every day." Yep, that's what started me on an unknown path. I had no idea what fears were going to show up, how I was going to handle them, what I was going to do. I just knew ONE thing: I was no longer going to let fear control my life.

I grew up in a volatile, abusive alcoholic household. When I was five years old, I ran away and was gone an entire week. I know what you're asking (it's always the first question people ask me), where did I go? I just went to the neighbor's house, so I was safe, but something happened that week that locked in a very strong belief about me and the people in my life.

There I was, five years old, and no one came to get me. What I didn't know is that my mom knew where I was the whole time. Why is this significant? Imagine that you are five years old and you decide to run away (most kids run away for fifteen minutes or an hour). You go to your friend's house and play all day long with your friend. You're having a great time. Then nighttime comes and no one tells you to come home. So, you stay the night at your friend's house. You're still having fun. The same pattern continues seven days in a row. Then, on day seven, your mom calls the neighbor and says, "Lynda has been gone long enough, you can send her home now."

Finally, your mom misses you.

What happened during those seven days was instrumental in my belief system for the next forty-six years, until the age of fifty-one (2015). The belief that was locked in tight to my core was "they don't love me; they don't want me around." Having this belief caused me to look at my life from that perspective, one of feeling unwanted and unloved.

When I came home, however, a whole different set of beliefs was created. I became riddled with fear and transformed into the ultimate people pleaser. I was a chameleon. I could adapt to any situation. If you loved it, I loved it. If you hated it, I hated it. I had a tremendous need to be liked. I remember saying, "I just want people to like me." So, I conformed to everything and everyone around me.

On that morning of January 1, 2015, I embarked on a journey like nothing else I had ever experienced. Rather than a New Year's Resolution, I decided to embark on a New Year's Commitment. A commitment felt so much better to me and simply changing that one word helped me grasp the gravity of what I was doing and it helped keep me on track. I decided that every morning I would follow a new routine. Every morning when I woke up, before getting out of bed, I would ask myself a simple three-word question: "What scares me?" Then I would lay in bed waiting for the first fear to hop into my head. My commitment to myself was to break through that fear that day.

What? Who does something like that? Who has that many fears? What types of fears showed up? Were any fears repeats? What did you learn? Was there an underlying fear?

I get asked those questions all the time. The main thing most people want to know is if I really had that many fears. They can't imagine breaking through fears 365 days in a row. Well, until that point, I couldn't imagine it either. As a matter of fact, I never did imagine it. It was just something that happened. Looking back on it, I believe it was my intuition telling me I had to do it so I could live the life I'm living now and serving my purpose on this planet. I had to break through those fears so I could take my position while I'm here.

The first three months I faced fears such as talking to strangers, starting a conversation, and going to networking events. I was feeling cautiously optimistic, but fear was still prominent. About three months into facing one fear every day, I was brushing my teeth and reciting an acronym I had heard many times in my life: False Evidence Appearing Real. False Evidence Appearing Real. False... Evidence... Appearing... Real. Staring at myself, I realized that acronym is a lie. I broke it down and realized that there was nothing false about my fear. My fears are as real as can be to me. There was no evidence in anything. It didn't appear real; it was real.

So, I looked over the previous three months and had this epiphany that when I tapped into my faith, it was much easier for me to break through my fear. You can't have faith and fear at the same time; they are opposites. I also realized that fear is nothing more than anxiety or nervousness, so I came up with my own acronym: Faith... Erases... Anxious... Reactions. When your faith is strong, your fear is weak. You just need to tap into your faith: faith in yourself, faith in others, and faith in God or your higher power.

I continued the process. Wake up, ask the question, wait for the answer, face the fear THAT DAY.

Over the next 90 days, I conquered fears such as asking someone to do something for me, speaking on stage, asking a celebrity to endorse my book.

After 180 days of fears, I looked back on the previous six months and asked myself a question, "What's the common theme between these fears? There's gotta be something." That's when I had another epiphany – the majority of my fears were caused by the fear of judgment.

Something as simple as starting a conversation with a stranger can be difficult for many of us. In my case, it was the fear of saying something stupid or ignorant. For others, it may be due to their speaking with an accent or not being an expert on a certain topic. Armed with this knowledge, I was able to tackle the next six months with a mission to rid myself of the fear of judgment. By the end of the year, judgment was no longer an issue for me. I did it.

One of the greatest lessons I learned during that year was that the vast majority of the time after breaking through my fears, I felt good about doing it, I was proud of myself, I met someone absolutely amazing that I wouldn't have met had I not broken through that fear, and that the results on the other side of fear were usually way better than I ever imagined. This was one of those mind-blowing moments that helped me realize that my fear was robbing me of what "could be." No more. I took a stand right then and there.

When my intuition spoke to me and gave me the idea to break through one fear a day for a year, had I not listened to that intuition, ignored it, and ran away (just like I did when I was five), I wouldn't have had the amazing experiences I've had. You see, I started to realize that I needed to break through my fears BECAUSE I was scared, not in spite of the fear, not feel the fear and do it anyway (those are disempowering statements).

When you break through fear **BECAUSE** you're scared, it creates an empowering feeling. I know that 99% of the time after I break through a fear the result is going to be so much better than I ever imagined. Read that one more time. 99% of the time after you break through a fear, the result will be so much better than you ever imagined. With that in mind, why would we deprive ourselves of the opportunities that are on the other side of our fears?

Some of the amazing things that have happened to me from breaking through my fears BECAUSE I was scared are:

- interviewed the President of Mexico in his Presidential Suite;

- interviewed hundreds of stars on the red carpet at the Academy Awards After Party;

- done over 6,000 live videos;

- became an Executive Film Producer of a movie called Wish Man, the story of the founding of the Make-a-Wish Foundation;

- became an Award-Winning 17 times #1 International Best-selling Author;

- met some absolutely incredible people who have helped me to continue transforming my life;

- and so much more.

The comfort zone is exactly like a balloon. Outside of the comfort zone is where opportunities and possibilities are waiting for you. The first time you blow up a balloon, it's kind of difficult. You have to puff up your cheeks and push a LOT of air into the balloon. Sometimes it makes your cheeks hurt. When you let the air out of the balloon, it has stretched out a little bit. The next time you blow up that same balloon, it's a little bit easier AND it gets a little bit bigger than the previous time. When you let out the air, it's a little bigger than it was the first time.

Just like the balloon, the first time you break through a fear, it's kind of difficult. After you've broken through that fear, you're a little less fearful prior to breaking through the fear. Sometimes you are elated with the results you got. The next time you break through a fear, it's a little easier. Not only that, but you have also enlarged the size of your comfort zone. The more fears you break through, the larger your comfort zone grows. Eventually you get to the point when you realize that breaking through your fears is crucial to your success, that breaking through your fears is necessary in order to live the life you truly want to live.

When we allow our fears to hold us back, we are not living our full potential.

When we allow our fears to hold us back, we are not experiencing everything this life has to offer.

When we allow our fears to hold us back, we are depriving ourselves of all the goodness that awaits us on the other side of fear.

I may not have the same fears as you, but our fears are very real... to each of us. Let's decide right here, right now not to allow anyone to rob us of our experience of that fear by telling us it's insignificant or ridiculous.

YOU have the power to break through that fear in that moment, but only you can make that decision. And it has to be a decision that you made FOR YOU, not one that someone else made for you.

Yes, fear is scary. But it doesn't have to control our lives. In fact, it can make life better. So, when you've identified a fear in your life, face it head on and do it BECAUSE you're scared.

LYNDA SUNSHINE WEST

She ran away at 5 years old and was gone an entire week. She came home riddled with fears and, in turn, became a people-pleaser. At age 51, she decided to face one fear every day for an entire year. In doing so, she gained an exorbitant amount of confidence and now uses what she learned to fulfill her mission of empowering 5 million women and men to write their stories. Lynda Sunshine West is the Founder and CEO of Action Takers Publishing, a Speaker, 17 Times #1 International Bestselling and Award-Winning Author, Executive Contributing Author at Brainz Magazine, Executive Film Producer, and Red Carpet Interviewer.

She believes in cooperation and collaboration and loves connecting with like-minded people.

Having grown up in a volatile, physically, mentally and verbally abusive alcoholic household and marrying someone just like her dad, Lynda's voice was stifled far too long. It left her feeling suppressed, ignored, and judged, which made her shut down.

At the age of 51, she found a life coach who helped her discover that she has value and that it was time for her to share her voice and speak out loud. In doing so, she was met with praise, recognition, and acknowledgment.

Lynda Sunshine no longer sits in the back of the room, but now speaks on stages, interviews stars on the red carpet, makes tv and podcast appearances, publishes books, and creates positive, uplifting, judgment-free safe zones.

Connect with Lynda Sunshine at www.actiontakerspublishing. com.

CHAPTER 3

Before I Lived, I Died
a Seemingly Thousand Deaths!

Karen Rudolf

My first near-death experience happened when I was a mere five years old after downing a bottle of nose drops. Having an out-of-body experience watching the medical staff work diligently over my frail body from one corner of the room, was quite unique and fun for a five-year-old!

Once more at twenty-one years old, I had one of those moments when I'm glad I wasn't following the law because not wearing my seatbelt saved my life!!

I hit a patch of ice, spun around, and hit a boulder dead on! The accident left my sports car with the long, sleek front smaller than a Volkswagen Bug by the time I came back into consciousness laying in a hospital bed!

You may have heard about the white tunnel effect when one passes; that was my experience! My journey upward had voices telling me to, "go back, go back, it's not your time, go back." It was not just any voice, however. It was a very distinct voice of my maternal grandmother who ha passed away five years earlier. I hadn't always been close with her life, so it was quite the surprise!

I've always believed that those of us who have near death experiences have been chosen for a higher purpose, something bigger than ourselves.

I continue to pursue the calling, a vision I felt deep within, because I believed I was being divinely guided, later to trust my intuition. This seems to me to represent the Spirit within, guiding me to a higher calling, my higher purpose to support raising conscious awareness and healing.

My modality… shifting perception from the inside out, as a light worker, wasn't something I stepped into readily. I went kicking and screaming at first. I didn't want the responsibility. When you're called, you're called, Period. Choosing to follow this calling has become part of my flow and finding my inner light, my GPS, my intuition, which guides me in the direction of my North Star.

Have you ever had a gut feeling about something and hadn't acted upon it? Doubting it, resisting? What was the feeling you were left with? What was the feeling you had when you *had* acted on it?

Since I was a little girl, I have had such inner feelings… knowings. Of course not knowing what they were or what they were about, I felt different than the other children I played with.

Often, I would merrily go alone to the end of the street and disappear into the forest to my favorite bush and crawl inside my "igloo." It was there that I healed my Barbie dolls with leaves. Even back then I knew and trusted I was healing them, but from what? I had no idea.

I knew things before they would happen. If I said something about it, I would be sent out of the room. I sensed that my mother and grandmother had what I thought was ESP; however, no one spoke of it.

When I met my former husband in my 20s, he was the first to ever mention that I was 'freaking him out' and he asked me to "turn it off." Turn what off? "*It*" had no label and he now freaked me out, thinking there was something wrong with me. After that, when things showed up for me, I'd shut down the thoughts and feelings, believing there was now something wrong with me.

After twenty-nine plus years of shutting 'It' off, I'd lost whatever 'It' was,… so I thought.

Sometime after my divorce, I was invited by a client to a creativity conference in Portland, Oregon. Up until that point, I had not met him in person; all of our sessions were over the phone. When I arrived, I had no idea for whom I was looking to connect with. So off I went in search of him.

As I was coming over the hill towards the community room, I suddenly froze and felt glued to the ground. I couldn't move. Behind me, a man named Joe, who later became a dear friend of mine, came up and introduced himself. I burst out crying. "What's wrong?," he asked. "I don't know," I replied.

Right on cue without skipping a beat, "I know just who to introduce you to. Follow me." Off we went to meet, as fate would have it, Kathy Brown, a Medical Intuitive from Chicago and as chance would have it, my roommate.

Back in the room, she had me lie down and go to work on, what she later told me was, my inner child being suffocated by an umbilical cord and she'd unraveled it just in time. I shared with her how I 'knew' I was a healer and felt like Harry Potter with a wand not knowing how to use it.

Empathetically, she'd mentioned she had a slight headache and asked me to do 'my magic' on her. I had no idea what I was doing other than to get still and move my hands as if guided by an inner knowing.

After, she mentioned she felt better, it had faded. She left and I stayed, pondering what had just happened. Shortly after, she returned and told me I had supported her headache disappearing as it actually did go away after she'd left the room. Could it be possible? Could I have healed her?

From that point on, I'd lay my 'healing hands' on anyone who would allow me to touch them. They all gave me positive feedback until... I was told that laying on hands was illegal. Being the 'rule follower' and people pleaser I'd become, I stopped, again believing it was wrong of me.

As I began my journey into self-discovery, I began owning my gifts. I became obsessed with Quantum Physics, Neuroscience, and World Religions searching for answers as to why I felt different. I'd never actually found them.

My rigorous study of Spirituality combined with science began answering many of my questions my curious mind had and things began making more sense. Every topic I studied had supported how I presently support others in my career path today.

One of the things I began to believe in my world was that if everything were Energy, and everything came to us in signs and symbols, for me, it then stood to reason that all the synchronicities which were unfolding in my life weren't just a fluke. Things began to make sense to my brain and how I might begin to apply these happenings into my life. As I began opening myself up to these new awarenesses, I began trusting the thoughts and meanings which came to me as an inner knowingness. I surrendered to the knowing, trusting them, embracing them, owning them.

I was getting my hair done one day and my daughter was impatiently waiting for lunch. As I looked across the room, there was a young, gaunt gal twenty-six-ish, struggling to open her Gatorade. My inner voice quite loudly spoke and said, "go over there and tell her she will be okay."

What? Where? Who said that? It repeated itself. As I went to move out of the chair, my daughter gave me a look as if to say, come on mom, I'm hungry. I looked back at the girl and froze. I felt embarrassed in front of my daughter, so I did nothing. Sadly.

Later, I'd mentioned it to my girlfriend as to how strong that calling was and she yelled at me, telling me I have been given a gift and I should be following these requests before it gets pulled away. "NOT AGAIN!!," I thought and made a vow to myself that I would never ignore the 'callings' again. Powerful lesson!

During my divorce, one of my horses got struck by lightning (Truman was the second of my horses to be struck). The vet came and recommended I put him down. 'Karen, you have young children, you're going through a divorce, and it will cost you a fortune to rehab him.'

I recall shutting my eyes, getting still, and taking a deep breath. As if downloaded, I shot my eyes open, looked him straight in the eyes and, without thought, spurted out, 'not only will Truman survive, he will thrive and he and I will become catalysts for change!'

I looked at him stunned as the vet looked at me wide-eyed. I had no idea where those words came from.

After two horses of mine were now struck by lightning and Scamper (my soul connection horse) died, my Spiritual Mentor asked me when I was going to look up the spiritual meaning of lightning strike. I told her I didn't have to as I already knew, I just hadn't wished to be responsible for that knowing. She laughed and said, "okay, when you're ready…" That's all it took.

Being struck by lightning means being a "light in the world."

Ugh, after Truman's recovery, I finally said 'yes' to being a Light Worker. Truman thrived and back in 2008 we became catalysts for change in the world.

During the time of Truman's recovery, my mother was not well. She was on nineteen medications and the three doctors hadn't collaborated on what meds she was taking.

When I called her one day, she began slurring her words. I dropped everything to go see her. On the floor, what I saw was a rather child-like version of herself in a ball. All she'd ever wanted was to be heard, loved, and feel like enough and hadn't known how to ask. Right then and there, with my newly vowed declaration to be a catalyst for change, I began the trajectory of who I was to become in the space of healing lives, following my inner guidance.

It was knowledge such as this that had me become a believer! I began trusting myself and that inner voice. The more I felt guided, the more I became of service to others and myself at the ripe young age of fifty. Seems to me it never matters the age of our calling. When we are called, we have the choice to follow or not. Not, still being a choice!

Being human, I have times when I don't always listen. I want to do it my way doesn't always work, in fact rarely does it… One particular time, my intuition was screaming at me, and I ignored it. I wanted to trust a man I'd met online. He wanted to become business partners and was so smooth and cool. He had a way with words. When he asked me to invest, I trusted him, and he ran off with my money. Should've, would've, could've listened and things would've been different! It was a very expensive lesson, but today I LISTEN more keenly.

After my divorce, many people kept telling me to go back into nursing, 'it's solid,' they said, 'you'll have a steady paycheck.' Blah blah, blah. Why would I do that? I knew I could make a difference in this holistic arena using the knowledge I'd gained in nursing and my other life experiences. This became my foundation to build on.

I refused to listen to the thoughts, feelings, and opinions of others and it allowed me to follow my own internal guidance. I love what I do!

I feel turned on and it lights me up! Although I enjoyed nursing and being of service to my patients, it wasn't the same internal feeling and glow I experience now. I wouldn't change it for the world!

Today, I support clients by creating a safe space to explore that which no longer serves, shifting traumas and stressors into living a fulfilled life filled with peace, harmony, and alignment.

I, too, live this life of choice. I like to call it a *Life by Design,* the name of my programs which support others discovering and being their authentic selves. There's nothing quite like finding that inner power of living an authentic, self-expressed life. Freedom lives there!

We all have intuition. It begins with being quiet and still long enough to listen, hear, act, and trust the guidance. By asking self-inquiry questions, the answers often come quicker. Intuition is *always* heart based. Act quickly before getting caught up in your head (the Ego) where all the monkey chatter happens along with the self-doubt which holds us back. Learning to stay in the heart is key.

It seems to me our intuition is our internal Superpower, our magic, our GPS system which guides our decisions, directions, as well as our personal growth and development. It always begins with child-like curiosity and wonder. Curious? You have the power within as well waiting for you to discover.

Following intuition allows distinctions of what to align with, what not to, as well as remaining here to the present moment. For that I'm always grateful.

KAREN RUDOLF

As a "W"Holistic Intuitive Journey Guide supporting personal transformation from the inside out, Karen Rudolf has taken a different approach to supporting her clients.

As a Transformational Specialist committed to being a catalyst for positive change, Karen has developed a process that supports her clients in uncovering where they are stuck, unraveling the truths about what they want so, ultimately, they can live a more fulfilled, more passionate, higher performance life while building a strong reservoir for empowerment.

Karen is a masterful guide to peaceful thriving. In each of her Tranquil SOULutions programs, your experience will be derived from a variety of natural, gentle, and delightfully entertaining modalities.

Karen continues to evolve in her own personal and professional transformation as well. With her licenses, certifications, trainings, and experiences, she's created a model for well-being and wellness in the areas of Mind, Body, Heart, and Spirit.

With a passion, she specializes in Heart-Based Mind shift journeying, with a "W"Holistic focus on Well-Being and a playful twist.

She is an Author of *5 Ways to Create A Ripple* as well as the collaborative international bestselling book, *Ignite the Entrepreneur*. She is a Speaker, Licensed Spiritual Healer, Practitioner, Nurse, Licensed HeartMath Practitioner, Master Practitioner of RIM (Reimagining Images in Memory), Bio-Well Practitioner, NLP Certified (hypnotherapy, timeline therapy as well), and is experienced in Equine Supported Sessions using the RIM method alongside horses.

In total, she has created a career in reengineering human perceptions.

Connect with Karen at www.TranquilSOULutions.com.

CHAPTER 4

Whispers of the Soul

Stacie Shifflett

"Don't put that there. You're going to knock it over and break it!"

"That car is going to cut in front of you...be careful."

"You might want to close the drain before you do that!"

I receive these kinds of messages all of the time. It's the little voice in my head that guides me in all things. When I listen, anyway. And at this point in my life, I generally listen. Why? Because I've learned that when I choose to ignore these promptings, I regret it as the thing gets broken, I have to perform a hasty driving maneuver to avoid a collision, or I drop the tiny, little piece in my hand and watch as it hits the counter once then bounces into the drain hole with the precision of a trick basketball shot that seemingly defies all odds.

But my intuition goes beyond these simple, albeit helpful, hints that are now part of my daily life. At times, I'm blessed with a profound 'knowing' or an idea, including some that seem outrageous, if not impossible, that completely change the trajectory of my life. I may feel the 'goosies' of energy surging through my body informing me that I am, indeed, on the right track when I have a thought or am working with someone in my coaching practice. Sometimes I'm guided to a thought intended for me to explore with the insight that this concept potentially holds a key to my next level of growth. And, occasionally, I receive information that prophesies the future.

I believe the sources of these promptings are as varied as the messages themselves. They may emerge from my subconscious to assist me at just the right time with reminders from knowledge I've gained through experience. My higher self, which I call 'my little voice,' may, among other things, prompt me to consider something. Or I may receive a message or interaction with a being from beyond this Earthly plane. That may sound like a bold statement, so let me share with you some personal experiences that prove, to me anyway, that something beyond the physical exists.

I was one of those kids that had an 'invisible friend' throughout the earliest years of my life. His name was George, and I can recall introducing my mother to him when she asked me who I was talking to! You see, she was hearing one side of what was obviously a conversation with someone. But with whom? When mom asked me if I could see him, I said "Yes, he's right there! Can't *you* see him?," as I pointed in his direction. My mom fully accepted this explanation with a "nice to meet you, George." She never doubted his existence and always acknowledged him by name. He went everywhere with me. One time, when my little hand was accidentally slammed in the car door smooshing my little fingers, George was there by my side soothing and consoling me along with my parents.

George was a constant companion for a couple of years, but I have no conscious memory of him by the time I started Kindergarten. As a matter of fact, throughout school I only have two profound memories of these types of encounters. The first was being awakened one night by something tapping me three times firmly on the forehead — thump…thump…thump. I was about eight when this happened and I remember laying there, eyes wide open, trying to figure out who had touched me as there was nobody in the room but me! My entire family was very ill at the time, all of us bedridden. It frightened me, but for some reason I didn't call out for help. In the morning, when I told my mom what had happened, she expressed gratitude as she had prayed during the night that an angel would heal me. I did, indeed, heal very quickly after that experience.

The second experience with an entity beyond the physical was when a presence entered my room late one night while I was in college. I could see him, a figure that appeared as a three- dimensional shadow, most definitely in the shape of a man, as he walked toward and then stood by my bed. The first time I saw him terrified me. I tried screaming, but I couldn't make a sound. I laid there completely frozen with fear, gazing at him eyes wide open. In a few minutes, he turned from my bedside and walked away, right *through* the closed door of my bedroom. I really did not know what to make of this situation! However, over time, he and I became friends of sort as we began to fully accept each other's presence and grew comfortable sharing the space of this home. Quite often I could hear his footsteps moving through the house after dark. Although he never communicated with me, he did begin to respond to me when I spoke to him. *Yes, you heard that right.* For some reason, rather than gliding through the door as if it didn't exist as he did the first time I saw him, he began to use the doorknob to enter my room during the night. As I would hear his footsteps approaching my bedroom, I would lift my head from my studies and gaze at the door. The footsteps would stop outside my door, the doorknob would turn and, as the door began to open, I would say, "Jimmy. Not tonight. I'm studying for an exam." And, with that command, the door would stop its forward motion, gently close fully, the latch locking into place, and his footsteps would continue walking the path they always walked as he gently faded away. Apparently, Jimmy had friends, too, as one night I was awakened by the sounds of a grand party, complete with voices and laughter and harpsichord music emanating from what was originally the salon in that historic house. That was interesting! Over time, he stopped visiting, much like George.

Now, consider this: do you think my experiences would be different had my family discounted my encounters with George as a child? What if they had told me that nothing exists beyond what I can actually see with my eyes? What if they had told me that it was silly and crazy to believe I had an imaginary friend? I think, even if I continued to converse with George, I would have learned to not speak of it to avoid being chastised. I also may have adopted the belief that there is nothing beyond what we can see with our physical eyes. If that were the case, would it have closed me to other 'unexplained' phenomena throughout my life? Would I have been rendered fearful instead of curious?

In my forties, I was gifted with the thought to acquire a software company valued at tens of millions of dollars. That idea certainly seemed outrageous and impossible as I had no money to acquire that company, but I followed my intuition with action and fully stepped into creating this reality. Throughout the process I believed, without a doubt, that not only *would* this happen, but that it was *meant* to happen and, guess what? I acquired that software company which, to this day, provided me with financial security. My situation would be remarkably different had I not followed that prompting, particularly given that my 28-year marriage ended shortly thereafter. Was it divinely timed? I think so.

A few years ago, I awakened one morning with the powerful idea to move to Sarasota, Florida. I'm originally from Florida, but I have no memory of ever visiting Sarasota, even as a child, let alone have any logical reason to relocate there. However, the message I received was strong and, believing it to be a divine prompting, I followed it with faith. Within two weeks, I was on a flight and put a contract on a home on beautiful Siesta Key, which is my primary residence today.

How is it that I came to a place in my life where I would literally move forward in faith, that I was willing to take action even if I didn't think that my situation at that time could support the idea? It's because I've developed my field of awareness to expand beyond my known world; that is, what I believe is possible for me, what I think I'm capable of, etc. In other words, I've learned through experience that possibilities far beyond my imagination are available to me. And, if they are possible for me, they are also possible for you!

I recently heard Michael Beckwith offer an analogy describing fields of awareness, or perception, with a story about an ant, its hole, and a grain of sugar. Imagine an ant standing halfway between two points: the hole on the top of the anthill it emerged from and a grain of sugar. From the ant's perspective, the hole is its past, the sugar is its future and its position between both is its present. There is time involved in that scenario; past, present, and future. Now imagine that we are standing over the ant gazing at its situation. To us, with our expanded view from a higher elevation, all of this is happening in the now — there is no past or future. We simply acknowledge that the ant is in the act of getting the sugar. This is the same in our lives. If we don't lift our perception — that is, expand our field of awareness beyond that which is immediately known to us — we may miss the bigger picture, which we often do as we humans run consistently on our programming. That's how we are wired! Ninety-five percent of our brain's activity comes from our subconscious programming, what we do automatically without thought; about five percent comes from our creative thinking mind. You can find many studies that support this. Our programming includes our beliefs, our conditioning, and what we regard is possible for us. Sometimes we think something may be possible for someone else but not for us based on our beliefs. For example, I could have easily succumbed to the conclusion that there is no way I could acquire a software company with no financial investment. But, I chose to ignore my programming and instead believed that I could do it.

We can all expand our field of awareness. We can all expand the possibilities in our lives. In order to do that, we need to step beyond the internal programming that is limiting our potential.

Lao Tzu said, "When I let go of what I am, I become what I might be." That's great, but how do we determine where we are today? Where do we begin? I'm not talking only about an assessment of where we are in terms of our physical situations — our careers, our families, our financial situations — although those are indeed things to consider. What I'm talking about is how to expand your awareness of what beyond the physical might be constraining your greatness, your beliefs.

This isn't a new concept. Perhaps you've read books on this subject, attended seminars, and already know this. But have you expanded beyond the intellectual knowledge you've gained and integrated the practices you've learned into your daily activities? Or do you continue to let your established programs do the heavy lifting in shaping your life?

I received a prompting a couple of years ago to create a company called Modern Consciousness™. The concept for the company flowed through me as did information on the current state of our world including a glimpse of the energies behind much of what we are experiencing today. It left me a bit dazed as the energies are quite dark and dense and the task of creating this company seemed improbable and not very desirable to me on many levels. I resisted the idea for a time for a number of reasons, but I finally surrendered. Had I not, you would not be reading about my story today.

In my theory of Modern Consciousness™, I see four primary stages of growth. The first stage I call 'automaton' and it is characterized by running on autopilot, much like a machine that is designed to automatically execute a pre-determined sequence of operations based on encoded instructions. This is a valuable stage in our lives as it creates our baseline. I call the next level 'illuminated skeptic.' To me this phrase doesn't mean someone who doubts possibilities, but rather calls to question the status quo of their lives. In other words, they become skeptical that the life they are living is all there is. People in this stage have a willingness to seek out information and learn with an open mind. Their appetite to explore the deeper meaning of life has been whetted and it's within this phase that we become what I call 'awakening souls.' It is here that we become aware that there just might be more available to us, and we begin to adopt and align to new beliefs. This leads us to become 'transformers' of our lives, where we continue to expand our knowledge, and when we begin to embody new behaviors that facilitate not only our personal transformation but also those within our orbit. There is not a linear progression through these stages. We flow between them.

I don't want to publish this story and leave you without something actionable to support your journey. I want to serve you in some meaningful way. An action you can take to begin unravelling the deep, tangled web of beliefs that comprise your subconscious — which means outside of our conscious awareness — is by bringing them *into* your conscious awareness. How? Create a habit of noticing what triggers you into a negative feeling and then explore why.

Think of it this way. Instead of viewing your emotional triggers as annoyances, view them as a treasure map that can lead you toward inner peace. Try to objectively observe your feelings in these situations. Do you notice any patterns of behavior or thought? Once you identify these things, begin questioning them to determine if they are supporting you in creating your best life. If not, guess what? You have the power to change it! Carry a little notebook and jot these things down during your day as you notice them. Then, consistently set aside time later in your day to reflect on these situations. Rather than being a faithful servant to your mind, question it! Also, learn to turn down the volume of your thoughts so you can hear your 'little voice' as I assure you, she is speaking to you!

As the philosopher Jiddu Krishnamurti said, "intuition is the whisper of the soul." Listen to the words gently being whispered into your mind and Elevate Your Life!™.

STACIE SHIFFLETT

Stacie Shifflett is the Founder & CEO of Modern Consciousness™, LLC. She is an Entrepreneur, Consciousness Coach™, and International Best- Selling Author.

Stacie is an accomplished businessperson and entrepreneur with experience and successes that span multiple industries. She is also a proficient student of life blessed with the gifts of insight, grit, and optimism wrapped in a heart full of compassion.

A life-changing event in 2012 propelled Stacie forward on a personal journey of healing and self- discovery. During this time, she created opportunities to study with some of the best in the world on a wide range of topics and modalities.

Her goal? To gain a better understanding of the human condition in general and, even more importantly, her own beliefs and mindset. That journey ignited in her a desire to help others reclaim their joy and peace of mind with the belief that we all have the freedom to fully align with the brilliance that is uniquely ours.

Stacie Shifflett founded Modern Consciousness™ in 2021. What is Modern Consciousness™? It is the ability to raise our awareness of unconscious processes habituated in the past in order to intentionally shift our current daily life from one overshadowed by inner turmoil and frustration to one rooted in internal peace and joy. Stacie believes that this is the secret sauce to a life well- lived.

Connect with Stacie at https://modernconsciousness.com.

CHAPTER 5

The Choices We Make

Batoul I. Ajlouni

"Can't believe I did this."

"I can't believe I did this!"

It's as if hearing my own voice repeating the words over and over again, in a myriad of melodies and emotions, is the only way to make what I have just done stick.

It's already dark as I get into my car. Nothing drastically unusual about the level of daylight, or the lack thereof, as I leave the office building this evening. The view from my windshield, however, seems slightly different. A little brighter maybe, a little wider.

"Which route do I take today?" I ask myself.

Doesn't matter much really, but I *have* to turn one way or the other. So, I decide to make a right.

There is a spot just around the corner where the street reaches a T. Nothing more than your standard intersection unless you happen to be there before sundown to catch one of the most spectacular air shows that takes place in the heart of the city. An area where the edge of the hilltop meets an open sky and birds soar in free play, circling up and down air-currents in a daily ritual to bid the sun farewell. Too bad I missed the act today. The mere thought of it as I reach that viewpoint lifts me up, like it manages to do every time I'm fortunate enough to be there before the curtain falls. Taking a left at the junction, I catch myself smiling while I drive down that same hill.

Stopping at the first traffic light, I lay my head back in a thoughtful moment. This time one of hope, instead of the usual despair I have lately become so used to.

"What will tomorrow bring?" I wonder. And I realize tomorrow will be the weekend. That obviously means that today is the last work-day of the week. What makes this day different, though, is that it also happens to be the last workday of the year, and, still not fully comprehending the situation I am in, today is, in fact, the last working day for me.

The choices we make!

The trees are almost done preparing for winter, giving away whatever remains of their hanging leaves to the soft wind blowing outside my windshield. Oh, how I miss being in the outdoors. Such a shame. Summer had come and gone once again, while I was busy fighting fires, helplessly suffocating behind closed doors. Not a good place for me, or anyone else, to be in, regardless of the season.

Red turns green and I drive ahead. A long stretch of the road takes me back thirty years to a place I have been thinking of a lot. A specific decision I made back then, that had pivoted my career path and kick started my entrepreneurial journey. I have been wondering what my life would look like had I not gone down that path. It was what I had wanted; to build my own company. I had no interest in climbing anyone else's corporate ladder. What I had wanted was to create a startup that would, one day, grow into a corporate business others could rise through. That became my goal, my life for three long decades, nonstop.

Until, one day, it all stopped. When a glimpse in a long-forgotten mirror reflected an unhappy, old, and tired soul who seemed to have been wearing my body for quite a while. A complete stranger looked me in the eye and said: I own you!

How, why and when that takeover happened is beyond me. At some undefined point in time during the past few years, my unbeatable drive and passion for work had started to drain out, and bit by bit, the fire I had in me, that same fire that had ignited my career life for decades, had started to *burn* me instead. Stillness had left me for good. All I've dreamed of ever since was the life I had missed out on. All I could think of was the continuous urge to break out of those prison walls. The same corporate walls I have spent half of my life building.

Sleep has been impossible, so is getting that exhausted body of mine out of bed every morning. Peace seems to have abandoned my soul the day anxiety came into my life and announced itself as my new ugly companion.

Enough.

The horrifying image I saw at that moment sickened me, and my new mission from that point on was to get my life back on track.

The choices we make!

That choice ranked quite high on the decisions-no-one-ever-wants-to-take scale, since it would, immediately and without mercy, catapult me onto a path no enthusiastic, successful, middle-aged workaholic would ever want to tread: the unknown. No work, no plan in mind, no drafted future, and no idea whatsoever of what my days would look like. I was frightened. I was confused. I was determined.

"Can't believe I finally did this!"

Change is simpler and less turbulent when we're young. Or at least, when we have some sort of destination in mind, regardless of how foggy or distant it may be. Or maybe the decision I actually made that day, the road I had chosen the moment I stood in front of my darkened reflection, truly deserved its rough rating. After all, it did mark the end of an era. That decision inaugurated the retirement of my career. Something no one's ever prepared for, I believe. But then again, what choices did I have? My life was at stake, my mind, body, and soul.

I reach another red light. Ah, rush hour. A much-underrated perk of working late day in and day out is that we get to skip the unforgiving routine of drive-back traffic. Doesn't bother me much today, though. I have nowhere specific to be and, for once, time is not an issue. So, I turn on the radio and relax. The DJ is hyped, understandably so. It is the festive season after all, and a new year is just around the corner. Happy, hopeful times, but I'm not there yet; so, I change the channel.

A man in the car next to me is on the phone having what appears to be a serious back and forth. A suit in an intense argument. Trouble at work probably, something that has become the norm for me in the last year or so.

Stop dwelling on the past! "It's over now," I tell myself. Ahh how can I? This has been my dream career. Thirty years of my life that I have just ditched!

How did it ever get to this point?

Wasn't I the one who created this? This was *my* dream, no one else's. Haven't I been fighting to spend every waking moment nurturing it, making sure that nothing would ever change its forward track? Hasn't this been my passion? My one and only priority in life?

When did it all turn against me? Where has my fire gone? What stole my energy, my hope, my heart? Who let that stranger in?

And who is that hypocrite into whom I have just turned? For years, I have been mentoring young entrepreneurs, advising them to put their careers ahead of everything else in life; family, friends, fun, and I was their living and breathing example. Nothing else mattered in my opinion until, one day, *everything* else started to matter. This role model broke.

"What will my tomorrow bring?" I wonder.

The traffic light changes, but I don't make it across in time.

Breathe!

I change the channel back to that lively station and turn it up a notch. Hopefully, my ever-enthusiastic DJ friend will help stop those draining thoughts of mine.

I know I have to start living the moment. Take my time doing things. Do things I enjoy. Be with the ones I love. Walk slower and, hopefully, sleep better. I start thinking of all the things I've always wished I had the time for. Family. Friends. Exercise. Travel. Catch up on my reading. Stare into nothingness or hike the world. Oh, and now I can finally get to that ten-thousand-piece jigsaw puzzle I've been dying to challenge myself with.

I am definitely not short on ideas about keeping busy. I have thirty years of catching up to do. However, I cannot help the feeling that's burning inside of me. The feeling of guilt, loss, and worthlessness. Who am I without work?

I need time to figure out the mess I've drowned myself in, and time is what I have plenty of at this point.

Red turns green again. I drive ahead and finally manage to make it through the traffic light.

A song about the power of magic comes up on the radio. Is it in my head?

Life is magical. Is it right for us to set it aside, ignore everything it has to offer and watch it all pass us by in the name of our careers?

Could the promise I made to myself in front of the mirror that day, that frightful decision I made, could it have been a magical one? Some sort of bitter yet inescapable choice that would eventually kick-start a whole new life for me; a sweet change, an alternate path and a different destination, even though I'm in my 'Dreaded-fifties?'

The choices we make!

The simple ones don't seem to register much in our heads, do they? Many, we even make subconsciously. It's those hard choices that leave their marks on our lives, and this one is undoubtedly up there. I hope it will save me; I need to be saved.

A new chapter in my life has just begun. A journey into the unknown. Is that a place I have planned to be in? Not in a million years. It is one I need in order to bring my old self back to life.

I turn right and take my last stretch uphill before reaching home.

Tomorrow is new. Tomorrow should be beautiful. Why not?

Tomorrow will be unlike any other day.

And now…

Over five years have passed since that day I took my last drive-back from work, but I feel I have grown younger, at least another five, in both body and spirit.

Life has much to offer. Beauty. Love. Adventure. We cannot afford to live on autopilot. Our dreams can change. Our priorities will always change and, for one reason or another, we may even find ourselves replacing old joys with new. And that's OK. That's the thrill of life and I'm now set on a path to explore it.

The trail I have chosen has not been the easiest but, so far, it has proven to be quite rejuvenating. Unexpected, to say the least. Packed with reflections and challenges and experiences I had neither planned nor anticipated. But that's where the adventure comes into play and this phase of my life has certainly been an adventure; a self-discovery and a re-creation of me in every sense of the word.

I am now on a mission to make up for the times I've missed, the joys I had given up, and the limitations I've lived through because of work, or rather, because of what I have allowed work to put me through. It all started out as a dream I aimed to fulfill, but I had pushed myself a little too far and, in the process, I had simply forgotten to live.

Healing doesn't come easy. Anxiety doesn't set you free in a day, or a week, not even in a year, especially when it's been holding you hostage long enough. I'm opening up to the world and to what it's throwing at me, but I'm also *creating* a new world around me, one that aligns in harmony with my new priorities and aspirations.

We burn out not because of too much work, but because of losing control over our own lives. We burn out because of not enough living.

At times, we need to let go of what has become our norm. To push ourselves away from our comfort zone and step up to new heights. We *need* to make those hard choices so that other opportunities can open up. Just like those autumn leaves we all love to watch. Those lives sacrificed so that the trees can survive the winter months. They let go in order to make room for a fresh start. For growth, for the life that awaits them when spring finally arrives. This is where I find myself today. I have survived the storm and let my old leaves blow away in the wind, ready for this new life of mine to sprout and blossom.

I have restarted my career and jumpstarted my life at an age many of us dread; and what a trip it has been so far.

I have ditched the success I spent half of my life building, to search for the passion I had lost somewhere along the way. In the process, I found a different breed of success, colored with experiences, achievements and rewards I had not expected. I have revived my ability, my capacity to learn again, to fail again. To restart. Discover those hidden horizons. Dream and excel and build something new. Yes, I have pivoted my entire being after fifty and I'm now crafting new opportunities for myself. Tapping into areas I didn't even know existed. Exploring what life has to offer and what I can bring to this world, yet again.

Creativity does not stop. Dreams don't stop. Our interests, our passion (and age) may change, but our drive for life should never stop. We all need purpose. We all have a spirited entrepreneur inside of us. We're human. It's in our nature to survive, to take risks, to create, learn, play and serve, to explore, love and wonder. The day we stop doing all that is the day we cease to exist.

Today is new. Today is beautiful. Today is unlike any other day.

BATOUL AJLOUNI

Batoul Ajlouni is the award-winning author of "Ditching Success?" She has first-hand experience with burnout mode, and had to make the most challenging career decision to save her life. She is an entrepreneur, a passionate workaholic, and a former business executive with many years of experience in fifteen of the world's toughest markets. She co-founded her company at the age of twenty-four, before serving as a senior business executive at a leading IT firm, helping it grow into a multinational corporation. Batoul Ajlouni lived to pursue her dream of professional success. Thirty years later, she reached the very height of her career, but the very lowest point of her life. Self-reflection and self-discovery helped her to move from work burnout to a life reinvented.

Batoul Ajlouni is now a writer and a life explorer, sharing her findings and transformational discoveries with audiences searching for answers.

Her memoir "Ditching Success?" has won multiple awards, and is available on Amazon.com.

Connect with Batoul at: www.BatoulAjlouniAuthor.com.

CHAPTER 6

The Dirty Little Secret of San Luis Obispo County

Debbie Peterson

When the editor called and said that I must be a hero in my hometown for standing up to political corruption, I laughed, "I am to some; to others I'm considered a liability."

I told her, "My true crime story, *The HAPPIEST CORRUPTION – Sleaze, Lies, & Suicide in a California Beach Town* sells out at local bookstores, but you won't see it on display. Retailers hide it in the back, afraid of backlash." Certain politicians, their devotees, the cannabis cabal, and the chamber of commerce exact a de facto ban of the book.

"They would prefer that the county not be seen in this light," I said. She exclaimed, "Oh, you're the dirty little secret of San Luis Obispo County!"

Sometimes, however, the secret gets out. Those in outside judicial or municipal positions occasionally let slip that SLO County is one of the most corrupt in the country. It's not something readily seen because, as Oprah said in 2011, our county seat, San Luis Obispo is the Happiest City in America. Indeed, it is a beautiful, idyllic place to live, away from the reach of state and federal agencies that might otherwise take notice. Nobody really knows nor wants to know. I can't say that I blame them; I didn't either.

In 2013, as the first directly elected female mayor of my town, and a successful businesswoman, I eagerly and systematically reviewed over 200 pages of reports on our sewer plant after three of its nine workers blew the whistle and lost their jobs. Activists and residents were furious following a big spill. The grand jury published a scathing report, and the water board was angry, too. I found myself feeling anger, disgust, frustration, horror, incredulity, and annoyance at the extent of the mismanagement.

I had owned a manufacturing company and worked as a management consultant, so I was equipped to do a management review, but when I asked for the sewer plant accounts, the board and administrator blocked their release in every way they could. After enduring six weeks of lies and stalling, I slammed my hand down on the table as we met in a restaurant and shouted, "I will not sit on a board on which I cannot see the accounts!" That did it. They looked around furtively to see who might have heard, made one more attempt to block my request, and provided me with the previous five years of accounts.

I couldn't believe my eyes. I didn't want to believe my eyes. For five years, on income of $3 million a year they passed budgets of $6 million. They drained $11 million of reserves to almost nothing. Legal bills were more than $400,000 a year. I found 40 red flags in my red flags analysis – issues arising from the accounts or unaddressed from previous reports. The agency needed to be reorganized and needed an in-depth audit of accounting methods and practices.

I didn't want to believe that there could be corruption in the little town that I loved. More than once I awoke in the middle of the night wrestling with the idea and every time going back to the numbers I had to conclude that the numbers didn't lie. It was there in black and white. I couldn't avoid it and I had to report it. I asked to agendize a discussion of reorganizing and auditing the sewer plant. I got the same runaround I'd received regarding the accounts. It took two months, but finally it was agendized.

The night I presented my red flags analysis there was standing room only in the chambers. The press and media came. I printed copies of the report for everyone and went through the report point by point. A friend recorded it all with his video camera. There was nothing the board could do but agree to reorganize the plant. They hired the expert I recommended. The administrator "retired."

It took another three years of consistent public pressure to get the audit. I recruited Carl Knudson, the IRS and FBI forensic auditor who chased down both the Oliver North/Noriega arms and drugs fiasco and the Colombian Medellin cartel's money laundering. Upon hearing that Knudson would be investigating, the sewer plant attorney resigned. Knudson's report, when submitted to the district attorney, resulted in the conviction of the administrator on charges of self-dealing.

A Pattern Emerges

Careless boards weren't new to me. Over the seven years I served as a councilmember, five of seventeen boards on which I served were so poorly run that if they were not corrupt they were wide open for it. One board was transitioning from private to government oversight. Two other women on the 12-member board were chief executive officers, as I had been, and we saw that the processes needed to be tightened up. We enlisted the support of a male board member, the publisher of the local paper, explaining what we were seeing, and the four of us convinced the board to make the needed changes.

As a councilmember, I had also served for two years, alongside the previous mayor and city manager as a chamber of commerce delegate.

I advocated for a city seat on the chamber board due to the high level of support the city provided the chamber. It was resisted but, finally after two years, my colleagues agreed and asked me to sit on the board. Within two months, the board admitted that the chief executive had been putting the bills in a drawer, not reporting them, and not paying them, and they were $32,000 in the hole. The chamber joined a neighbor chamber that assumed the debt. (Do you see a pattern here — women demanding best practice, improving financial reporting, rooting out corruption?)

After my mayoral term ended, a large group of concerned citizens funded Knudson to investigate the fourth of the five slipshod agencies, the Integrated Waste Management Authority. That attorney also "retired" when Knudson came calling. Knudson found more than half a million dollars of credit card receipts at the mayor's house, many appearing to be personal. The mayor was the president of the board and led the board in resisting an audit, claiming there were "no improprieties" while the agency resisted releasing public records for years until Knudson (successfully) sued for their release. The agency had to pay his court costs. The clerk of the board moved to Tennessee. The District Attorney charged her with embezzling over $25,000 and destruction of documents. She shredded so many records that there was not enough evidence for the DA to charge anyone else with crimes.

Meanwhile, my city council decided to be the first in the county to allow cannabis dispensaries. This was during a two-year period after I had lost a bid for another term as mayor to a former mayor who cheated in campaign reporting (and was fined by the Fair Political Practices Commission). Two years later, I was re-elected to the city council. The council crafted good ordinances, building in clauses that reassured the public…no change of ownership without council approval, background reports on owners and staff, annual licensing, requirements for accounting and security software that would be compatible with and connect with city and police departments, state of the art solar energy installations, and abandoning septic to hook up to sewer systems. Five years later, almost none of that has happened and many of the clauses have been changed, amended, or simply ignored. Three dispensaries opened. None were local cannabis distributers with clean background reports. Licenses were only granted to dispensaries with principals or close associates with felonies in their backgrounds.

After opening, the owners of two of the three dispensaries have been convicted of or charged with felonies. One is serving a jail sentence, in part for bribing the county supervisor referenced as the suicide in the title of my book mentioned at the beginning of the chapter. The corruption was so extreme that nothing that came before the council was clean. I resigned in 2019 explaining why, and when interviewed by the press and media said that the word on the street was that it was $100,000 to the mayor to open a dispensary. Two years later, the FBI issued a press release with that same information – a bribe of $100,000 offered for a dispensary. The FBI is still investigating.

Many of us wrote to elected representatives, judicial and law enforcement agencies, and the press and media at the state and national level asking for their help, to no avail. So, I took up my pen and began to write, in the hopes that a best seller could achieve two things: 1) attract the attention that might herald an era of clean government and 2) encourage people in other communities to participate in local government to ensure that their community did not become the next happiest corruption in America. And now I hope that this quick romp through some of my experiences and the statistics that follow will inspire a third: bring more women into office.

Here are some compelling reasons to do that:

1. It goes without saying, but I am going to say it, when **51% of our population is represented by only 28% of our public**

servants, that's just Wickedly Stupid, Women! The United Nations reports that we are #73 out of 140 nations. Who ranks better? Rwanda, Cuba, Nicaragua, Mexico, and the United Arab Emirates to name a few.

2. **Female leadership in political decision-making processes improves the output.** Research on local councils in India discovered that there were 62% more drinking water projects in areas with women-led councils. Norwegians found a direct causal relationship between the presence of women in municipal councils and childcare coverage.[1]

3. **Women Compat; they don't Compete**. The UN reports that women work across party lines through women's caucuses — even in the most politically combative environments.

4. **Fewer women engage in white-collar crime.** In his 2002 white paper on combatting government vendor fraud, Carl Knudson wrote that 75% of government fraud is carried out by men. EM Broker conducted a gender breakdown of defendants in financial scandals from 2001 – 2018 and found that 7% of those involved were women.[2]

5. Study after study shows that **boards with women are financially sounder.** This is now so well known that it doesn't need documenting.

6. **Countries run by women experience better health, less crime, and less destitution.** Recent studies corroborate this. The earliest North American example is the Iroquois Confederacy Great Law of Peace of five native American nations, the constitution of the oldest living participative democracy on

earth, established in 1142.[3],[4] The information in the section that follows is graciously provided for free and open access by the University of Oklahoma College of Law Digital Commons and the *American Indian Law Review*. The US Constitution modeled The Great Law of Peace in all but two precepts: the seventh-generation principle that leaders must consider the effects of their actions unto seven generations, and the leadership role of women.[5] Clan Mothers are the most respected members of Iroquois society and hold the highest positions of authority and they manage the public treasury. They appoint chiefs and depose them if they do not serve the public trust. Theft, hunger, and destitution were unknown among the Iroquois.[6]

Former U.S. Commissioner of Indian Affairs, John Collier, wrote, "the Iroquois wrought a social institution, a system of greatness of human relationships, a system for evoking maximum genius and for socializing it, and a role of women in society which well may stand today as the most brilliant creation in the record of man."[7] If the tenets of equality of the Iroquois Great Law had been adopted by the U.S. system, the status of women in America would have been radically altered. It has

3 The Editors of Encyclopaedia Britannica. (2018, Oct. 4). Iroquois Confederacy. Encyclopedia Britannica. Retrieved November 30, 2018

4 Johansen, B. E. (1995). Dating the Iroquois Confederacy. Akwesasne Notes New Series, 1, 62-63. Retrieved November 30, 2018

5 Renée Jacobs, *The Iroquois Great Law of Peace and the United States Constitution: How the Founding Fathers Ignored the Clan Mothers*, 16 Am. Indian L. Rev. 497 (1991), https://digitalcommons.law.ou.edu/ailr/vol16/iss2/5

6 Father Joseph Lafitau, who spent considerable time among the Iroquois, summarized the position of women with more clarity

7 J. COLLIER, Indians of the Americas 120 (1947).

been noted that the subjugation of colonial women was not entirely dissimilar from the way slaves were treated.[8] Women were classed as "chattel," the personal property of men. Upon marriage, colonial women could not sue, be sued, enter into contracts, make wills, keep their earnings, or control their property. A man could chastise his wife, restrain her freedom, beat, and rape her.[9] Colonial women had many duties, but no rights apart from the protection their husbands or fathers might deem fit. In contrast, Iroquois women had many rights and duties, and received great respect. Both Benjamin Franklin and Thomas Jefferson believed that an Iroquoian-style culture provided more opportunity for happiness than a European model.[10]

7. **People in nations with higher numbers of women in power report being happier.** The five Nordic countries – Finland, Denmark, Norway, Sweden, and Iceland – have all been in the top ten in each United Nations World Happiness Report and their parliaments are composed of 44% women. The Nordic countries come out on top on most global scales: the state of democracy and political rights, lack of corruption, trust between citizens, felt safety, social cohesion, gender equality, equal distribution of incomes, Human Development Index.[11]

---

8 C. Horowitz & M. Weissman, A HISTORY OF WOMEN IN AMERICA (1980).

9 Law, Founding Fathers, supra note 71, at 25.

10 Letter from Thomas Jefferson to Angelica Schuyler Church (Sept. 21, 1788), reprinted in The Papers of Thomas Jefferson 623 (J. Boyd ed. 1956)

11 The Nordic Exceptionalism: What Explains Why the Nordic Countries Are Constantly Among the Happiest in the World | The World Happiness Report

The other countries regularly found at the top of international life satisfaction scales – Switzerland, the Netherlands, New Zealand, Canada, and Australia – share the same traits: high quality non-corrupt state institutions able to deliver what they promise, are generous in taking care of citizens in various adversities, with a well-functioning democracy where citizens feel free and trust each other and their government institutions. These are things that women excel in. As Jefferson noted in 1809, "The care of human life and happiness, and not their destruction, is the first and only legitimate object of good government."[12]

Do you want to make the world a better place? The average American pays more than half a million dollars in taxes over a lifetime. Do you want the half million dollars you pay in taxes over your lifetime put to good use? Are you concerned that Social Security will run out of money in the next few years? Do you want honest politicians?

If so, elect women. Ladies, run for office. Be wickedly smart and make it work as only you can do.

DEBBIE PETERSON

Debbie Peterson was the first directly elected female mayor of Grover Beach, California, after serving as a city councilwoman and planning commissioner. Debbie chronicles those years in her Amazon #1 New Release, *The Happiest Corruption: Sleaze, Lies, and Suicide in a California Beach Town*.

Before her government service, Debbie helped her mother launch The Brownie Baker, baking handmade family-recipe cookies, and expanded her mother's concept into a successful bakery, cafes, and trucking and distribution outlets in Scotland and London. By 1992, the company had annual sales of $7 million and one hundred employees.

The Scottish Association of Master Bakers deemed her a Scottish Master Baker, and she was the 1992 Clydesdale Bank Scottish Young Business Personality of the Year, winning other business vision, training, and efficiency awards, including one from prime minister Margaret Thatcher.

Her first book, *The California Cake & Cookie Cookbook*, sold in Border Books, Barnes & Noble, and Harrods. She was a sought-after speaker at women's and business conferences and universities and consulted for development agencies, helping business startups and manufacturers in business planning, marketing, and restructuring. The Scottish Development Agency commissioned her to write Great Scotswomen in Business. She was featured in industry, business, and women's press and media, including BBC TV, The Sunday Times, Financial Times, Company Magazine, and House & Garden.

Debbie studied journalism and radio-TV at California State University, Fresno, before completing a BSc in communications (public relations) at the University of Idaho and an Entrepreneurship course at the Scottish Business School.

Connect with Debbie at https://debbiepeterson.com.

CHAPTER 7

I trusted, I Made the Leap, $50,000 Fell Out of the Sky, I Found My Life's Work and the Man of My Dreams (plus a happiness and contentment I never imagined was possible)

Debra Stangl

In January 1999, right around the time of my 47th birthday, I was at a real low point in my life. Every single part of my life was a mess.

I hated my work. I had just started my 20th year as a divorce attorney in Omaha, Nebraska, and it was just so negative, fighting with the other attorneys and being surrounded by mostly unhappy and heartbroken people. I loved the part where I was helping my clients, but that only felt like about 10% of what I was doing.

I was in a bad marriage.

I was more than 40 pounds overweight.

I was $50,000 in debt from some bad business decisions my husband, Tom, had made, but for which I was responsible because we were married. That debt weighed so heavily on me. By this time, we had been under the debt for over five years and, no matter what I did, I couldn't seem to make it go away. I would take on more cases, economize, etc., but nothing ever seemed to make a dent in it. I would wake up in the morning and go to bed at night with a knot in my stomach about it. Even worse, five years later Tom had started another business and was in the startup phase, not yet producing any income.

During those five years, I would meditate and pray and say, "Dear God, I'm so unhappy, please tell me what to do." Occasionally, I would hear a very small voice that would say to me, "you need to leave your law practice." Whenever I would hear that voice, it would actually make me angry, "How can I possibly leave my law practice? I'm $50,000 in debt, I have no money in savings, I'm our sole support, how can I possibly leave my law practice?"

What I failed to understand at the time was that this was my Intuition giving me the exact information I needed for my highest good. I just wasn't listening.

Let me explain. We all have a High Self, that highest part of ourselves which is directly connected to the Divine. I believe our Intuition is the means by which our High Self communicates with us. Our High Self is giving us information all the time, about things big and small, about things that are important as well as what we don't think are all that important (until we don't listen to the nudge of "get off at this exit" and suddenly we're stuck in traffic). That information can come to us in all kinds of ways – a feeling in your gut, a tiny voice, dreams, coincidences, synchronicities, the right person or book or information showing up at exactly the right time, etc. The key is to listen. I simply wasn't listening. And things just kept getting worse and worse (which is exactly what happens when we don't listen).

I was unhappy and miserable. I felt lost and completely stuck. I was so depressed that there were days I could barely drag myself out of bed and the only thing that made me get up was that I had a court hearing scheduled and I was required to show up. I must admit there were a few times I seriously thought of suicide, but I didn't have the nerve to follow through with it.

I was attending weekly sessions with a therapist who was an energy worker and she became very concerned about me. She also did kinesiology. When we muscle tested, it said that I should go on a retreat for seven days. "There's no way I can leave my law practice or spend the money for seven days," I told her, so we agreed that I would go somewhere and stay for three days.

When I was trying to figure out where to do a retreat, I suddenly heard the word "Sedona" in my head. Again, my Intuition was giving me a clue. I had heard of Sedona, but I had never been there, and I didn't even realize it was in the Arizona mountains.

Through a strange set of coincidences (again, my Intuition at play), I found a woman who had a small retreat center outside of Sedona. Ranjita asked if I wanted to do any sessions with her while I was staying there and I told her no. I really shouldn't have been spending the money on the retreat, much less doing sessions.

But when I got there, Ranjita and I sat in front of the fire and talked, and I told her about my situation. At one point she said, "your law practice is sucking the life force out of you." "Something" inside me told me to forget about the money and do the session. Again, my Intuition showing up and giving me a very valuable nudge.

The session was truly extraordinary. I've always had a huge connection with ancient Egypt and during the session Isis, the winged Mother Goddess, appeared in a vision. She lovingly wrapped her wings around me and told me everything would be okay, but then she said, "if you don't leave your law practice now, you're going to die like your mother did."

Oh, my Goddess. This time I got the message. I quickly realized that I was exactly the age my mother was when she had gotten sick and died five years later from cancer. She had been completely devastated by my father's alcoholism and infidelity as well as the financial destruction all that had wrought. She was devoutly Catholic and felt she couldn't get a divorce. She was unhappy, frustrated, felt stuck and hopeless. I have always believed she left him the only way she could – she got sick and died. It was an unconscious choice, to be sure, but a choice, nonetheless.

I saw how I had put myself on the same path as she. I felt all the things she had felt -- unhappy, frustrated, stuck and hopeless.

Now I could see that I had the same choice, but my choice was going to have to be a much more conscious one. Did I want to live, or did I want to die?

I knew I definitely wanted to live, but I didn't see how I could possibly leave my law practice. None of it made sense. If I left my law practice, what would I do? I had no ideas for any other way of bringing in money to support the two of us. I spent the next two weeks trying to figure out with my lawyer brain how I was possibly going to leave my law practice when we were $50,000 in debt, we had no money in savings, and I was our sole support. I added and subtracted, but I couldn't figure anything out.

During this time, I was doing a lot of praying and meditating. I was also asking God for help, but this time I wasn't begging or complaining, I was simply reaching out. Suddenly, there was a day when I had finished a meditation where I had asked to be shown what I was supposed to do. I was overcome with a knowing, an energy that filled my entire body. It felt like nothing I had ever experienced before. Along with this knowing came a feeling of trust that filled me completely. Next came this huge wave of gratitude.

I was weeping as I got on my knees. The deep knowing of my Intuition had completely filled me. "Okay, God, I get it that I have to do this and I'm going to do it," I promised God. "If it means selling the house and selling one of the cars and living in the other one and never going anywhere again (I love to travel, so that would have been a hard one) okay, I'll do it. But you've got to give me some help here."

Less than eight hours later I got a phone call from one of my former clients. At the end of the conversation, he told me that he had just bought a new mortgage refinancing business. I asked him if it would be possible to re-finance my house to get a lower monthly payment. He called me back in 10 minutes and said, "I can cut your mortgage payment in half, plus I can get you $50,000 in cash."

I had never told him (or anyone else) that I was $50,000 in debt because I was ashamed of it. Suddenly, in an instant, the weight of five years of worry was gone. It was gone within eight hours of asking God for help. It was gone within eight hours of going into that deep place of surrender and listening to my Intuition. I asked, I listened, I made a decision, and I got exactly the help I needed.

And that was just the beginning.

I spent the next three years going back and forth to Sedona for a month at a time to do deep healing work. I thought I would only be able to leave my practice for one year, but Tom's new Internet marketing business started taking off and he began supporting me both emotionally and financially, for which I am eternally grateful.

Suddenly, in 2001, three weeks before 9/11, I was in Sedona doing a session in the same room where my High Self had appeared to me in a vision almost three years before. My High Self came in again as Isis, and this time she said, "It's time to move to Sedona." I responded,

"Why? What am I going to be doing in Sedona?" I got no response. One of the things I have learned over the years is that the High Self doesn't usually show you the complete picture, only the next step. Mine had shown me the next step.

My brain started kicking in, telling me how crazy it was to move to Sedona. It made absolutely no sense from a financial standpoint. Tom had gone to work for his largest client and had a great job in Omaha (along with health insurance and stock options), and I had no idea what I was going to do in Sedona. But over those previous three years of doing all the work I had done on myself, the one thing I had definitely learned was how important it was for me to listen to my Intuition and do what I was being told.

Within 24 hours of receiving that message, I got a phone call from one of my new Sedona friends who said, "I hear you're moving to Sedona (Note: I had not told anyone I was moving to Sedona). I'm leaving for India for six months to film a documentary. Would you like to rent my house?" It's a fabulous house, and the rent offer was almost too good to be true. I said yes.

I went back to Omaha. Tom was excited about moving to Sedona and loved it there. We put our house on the market and it sold in three days (the real estate agent had said that it would take six months) for more than what the real estate agent had predicted. I took that as another sign that following my Intuition was the thing I had to do.

We moved to Sedona, and I sat there for six months awaiting some insights, but nothing transpired. I would pray to God and say, "I did what you told me to do. I came here. Now what?"

Suddenly, over those next few months, I started having dreams about what would become my work, Sedona Soul Adventures. I knew that dreams are another way our High Self and our Intuition brings information and answers to us, so I started paying close attention. In the dreams, I was being shown that over the past three years I had worked with so many extraordinary healers in Sedona and, perhaps as importantly, I also knew which ones weren't that great. I saw how it was the private, one-on-one sessions and not group workshops that had made all the difference. I remembered how I had told certain friends who wanted to come to Sedona, "You should do a session with this person and this person and stay at this place and be sure to have dinner at Dahl & DiLuca." On a very small scale, I was already doing it. My Intuition had shown me my path and was telling me what to do.

That was twenty years ago. Since then, we have helped tens of thousands of people with our private, custom-designed retreats. Individuals leave happy, content, and at peace knowing their life's purpose and ready to live it. Couples are able to let go of the resentments of the past, rediscover the love that brought them together in the first place, and bring the sizzle back into their relationship. It's ironic to me that I was a divorce attorney for twenty years, and now I've spent another twenty years doing so much to save and renew countless marriages. Hopefully the karma is balanced out by now! Even after all these years and helping thousands of people, I'm still amazed at what happens.

We even teach an online class now on *"How to Connect with Your Intuition"* because I know what a difference following my Intuition has made in my own life.

Over the years, I've had many people say to me, "Oh, you must have been so brave leaving your law practice. That must have taken so much courage." I never felt brave; I never felt like I was doing anything out of the ordinary. I was simply listening to what I was being told and then doing what I was being told. It took me five years to finally start listening, but once I started listening, each next step just seemed like the logical thing to do.

The icing on the cake was with my own love life. Tom and I amicably ended our 20-year marriage in 2010 and he is now happily living in Bali (he became a first-time father at the age of 60!). I was happily single for six years until something happened that made me realize I wanted to bring in a true soul partner, something I had never had before. I used the principles we teach at Sedona Soul Adventures and did sessions with many of my Practitioners to eliminate any blocks to bringing that in. I utilized the processes I talk about in my book *The Journey To Happy – How Embracing the Concept That Nothing Is Wrong Can Transform Your Life* to manifest the perfect connection.

In November 2016, I was sitting with my sister sipping champagne and watching the sunset at the Del Mar Hotel on the beach in Santa Monica, California. I had just taped an episode of a reality show for singles looking for their soulmate (teaching them how to remove energetic blocks such as "I'm not loveable" to bring in their perfect partner), when I received a ding from Match.com that someone had liked me. I had been on Match the entire six years since my divorce and never found anyone who I had more than a cup of coffee or glass of wine with. I looked at Richard's picture and felt a hit. Then I saw that he lived in San Jose, California, and I felt an immediate disappointment. After my previous long-distance relationship, I had decided I didn't want to do that again, so I had made the decision to not even respond to anyone who was further away than Phoenix, Arizona. I found that if I even engaged enough to say "I don't want a long-distance relationship" it would start this back and forth of communication that usually ended negatively, so eventually I just stopped responding at all to those people, even though it felt a little rude.

I showed his picture to my sister and she said, "he's cute." I read his profile where he focused on his work and his spirituality. My Intuition kicked into overdrive. I literally could hear a voice telling me to respond to him and forget about following my rule because he was so far away. I thought to myself, "for this one, I'm not going to be rude." I sent him a message back "You look great, but you're in San Jose," with my rational brain thinking that would probably be the end of it.

But it wasn't the end, it was the beginning, and one year later we married in Sedona, surrounded by the red rocks and friends and family and my Practitioners. Every step of the way I listened to my Intuition and am I ever glad I did! It has brought me the work of my dreams, my soul partner, and a happiness I never imagined was possible.

It's all available to us if we will:

Ask

Listen

Act

DEBRA STANGL

Debra Stangl is an example of how life is full of second chances. After practicing law for over 20 years in Omaha, Nebraska, Debra had a spiritual re-awakening in Sedona, Arizona, in 1999.

After moving to Sedona in 2001 and founding Sedona Soul Adventures in 2002, Debra developed the unique process of deeply transformational private retreats that are custom-designed for individuals and couples (not groups), utilizing over 60 of Sedona's Master Practitioners. Sedona Soul Adventures was named "Best of Sedona" for Retreats in 2020, 2021, and 2022, named "Best Marriage Retreats in the US" 2017-2022, "Best Couples Retreats Around the World" 2022 by Bride's Magazine, and has been featured in USA Today, The Today Show, The Washington Post, Forbes, Elle, Yoga Journal, and was named to the Inc. 5000 List of Fastest Growing Private Companies in the United States in 2019. Debra also leads group trips each year to Egypt and Machu Picchu.

Over 20 years ago, Debra developed a unique process called Transformational Life Coaching, which combines traditional forms of personal coaching with Intuition and vibrational alignment. She is the author of the #1 International Best Seller "The Journey To Happy – How Embracing The Concept That Nothing Is Wrong Can Transform Your Life"; co-author of "Dancing In the Unknown" with Becky Chasse (producer of "What The Bleep Do We Know?"), and co-author of the #1 International Best Seller "Awakening The Amazing In You" with Janet and Chris Attwood (authors of "The Passion Test").

Connect with Debra at www.SedonaSoulAdventures.com.

CHAPTER 8

Intuition: The True God Particle

Dr. Bee Thomas

Right from the beginning I want to assure you that you are all intuitive.... You were born with a unique genetic blueprint, and within that blueprint is a particular and unique intuitive style.

~Lauren Thibodeau, Natural Born Intuition

My intuition developed while I was yet in the womb. It came from the seeds of my parents, and beyond them, it came from the galaxy of the unknown. My intuition came from an all-knowing place, what some within the church world would call the Holy Spirit or God. My intuition developed before time and therefore is unlimited. It is unnamable.

I knew I wanted to be born on this earth. I chose my parents, including my biological father, who went missing after my conception. I chose my mother, who out of understandable desperation almost aborted me. She was young. My intuition brought me into this world. It told me I needed to be here at this time. My intuition was within my body. My body was created with an all-knowing intuition.

So, what is intuition? Google's English dictionary by Oxford Languages defines intuition as "the ability to understand something immediately, without the need for conscious reasoning." Synonyms for "intuition" are "sixth sense," "clairvoyance," "instinct," and "second sight" (Google's English dictionary , 2022). Albert Einstein described intuition as a useful and necessary part of scientific discovery (Thibodeau, 2005). Intuition is essential. It is a gift. A quick internet search on the topic will produce countless articles and debates on this subject-some suggesting you were born with it, others suggesting you shouldn't always trust it, and others teaching you how to develop it.

I never had to be convinced of this invisible world. I was amazed by energy in my early years. I've always known my intuition as a gift. I was born perceptive. I arrived with colic; the ancestors cured my colic by activating my higher self, which contains my intuition, by blowing pure tobacco smoke up my nose. The blowing of smoke is an ancient tradition, used by many Indigenous tribes. The Houma tribe, an ancestral southern Louisiana tribe, understands a baby with colic to be feeling the pains of the mother within the womb (Pitre, 1998). My pregnant eighteen-year-old mother did the best she could to take care of both of us while I was incubating in her womb, and my intuition felt her love, joy, and pain within the womb. My intuition knew my path, and I gladly came anyway. Our intuition is relentless. It is with us on this life path and beyond.

When we begin a conversation about our intuition, we might start with examples of times when we had opportunities to listen to our gut, didn't, and regretted it. We have all had those experiences, yet what I find intriguing about my own life is that I was born with a deep understanding of hearing and trusting the still small voice inside of me. I was born with spiritual understanding. The old folks used to talk about being "born with a veil." I was channeling information as a child in the '80s, I had visions of things yet to come, visions of things past, and visions of things hidden in plain sight. I had many spiritual insights and dreamt a lot of colorful, vivid dreams. Many of us have done the same in all generations. Often this channeling of information starts as children. Children are more open to the unseen because they are more connected to the unknown. Babies can see clearly. They can see energy. Babies trust what they see because their logic is not fully developed. They are pure beings. We can learn from children; they can teach us about our God-given intuition. They trust themselves until they are taught not to, or else they are encouraged to develop their intuition, as I experienced.

Over the years, through meditations and practicing stillness, I have had many revelations and epiphanies regarding my birth, the energies felt within the womb, and energies I've come to heal within this life-time. As a child, I knew that I was born unique and that we were all one being. I knew I was born with a gift, and that was the gift of sensing beyond what was present and trusting that feeling. I knew I was born with the gift of love, which, as I grew up, was confirmed and tested through various life experiences. We each have this gift of love. Love is why we are here. Trusting, hearing, and listening to your highest vi-bration, which is love, is the best thing you can do for yourself and the world. My mother told me when I was child that a gift ran within our bloodline and it had been passed down to me. No other information was given, yet as a child, I knew about a world that was beyond this tangible world. I understood that gifts could be passed down and that the universe could decide to awaken whoever wanted to be awake.

There were times in my life when I would pray for my gift to go away. I didn't want to see. Then I learned that I could control what I saw. I learned that I could indeed step away from my intuition. I could choose to go against my intuition. I could pick it up and put it down at will. However, I learned early on that my intuition guides me and goes before me no matter what path I choose. It never leaves me. Your intuition is your personal guide (Thibodeau, 2005). I knew to trust in the unseen. I trained to hear things unsaid. My ability to see, or what some call clairvoyance, developed before my hearing or clairaudience. I also developed my Claircognizance as a youth by reading the minds of my fellow students on the yellow school bus, on my way to elementary school. Later on in life I began to develop my spiritual sense of smell, and taste, as my dreams became more vivid. I can also remember times I've smelled things while awake that were spiritually symbolic. Your clair senses are part of your intuition. I've always had intuitive gifts that developed early. My gifts continue to develop as I experience life and learn to trust myself. I've always felt the energy of the unseen within my intuitive world.

I am not the only one with these stories. All beings come with a sense of knowing, which is intuition. Think of how many times you thought about someone and they called, or you had a feeling that you shouldn't attend an event and were later relieved that you didn't, or perhaps you felt inspired to attract money to your life and within the next few days your business partner was inspired to deposit several thousand dollars into your bank account. Your intuition is powerful and is present at birth. We are born with the all-knowing within us. All the spiritual libraries and holy sites that exist or ever will exist are within your DNA. All is connected, we are not separated from anything in the world. We are born whole because we are part of the all. Life is a circle. If we remember time is not linear but circular and if we recall that time is also an illusion and can be manipulated, then we will remember to trust ourselves. We will remember our intuition.

I was born with a fascination for space and the stars. I was throwing salt over my shoulders by the age of eleven and telling my mother hair-raising "stories" at three-years-old. As a toddler, I often sat with my grandmother, rubbing her hands, and singing. At five-years-old, I didn't know my grandmother had arthritis or what that meant. I simply knew that it pleased her to have her hands rubbed, and it made me happy to sing to her and sit with her. I knew that what I was doing had great value. I was attuned to the healing energy of the invisible. Your intuition is your presence. I trusted that part of myself when I was only five-years-old. In adolescence, my connection with insects, trees, extrasensory perception (ESP), reading palms, and other occult science enhanced my curiosity about this invisible world. The more I tapped into what I knew, the more natural I felt. The few people I have spoken to about these experiences could often relate. It is fascinating how we are constantly attracting our tribe. Your sacred intuition is so powerful that it will guide you like a magnet and tell you when to look out ahead!

I remember having a dream at around fifteen-years-old that startled me awake, and I clearly heard the words coming from my radio, "Angels save lives!" I did not recall turning the radio on. I heard no other words from the radio. The timing and clarity all made me pay attention. I acted on my intuition in response to the dream and the radio message. I contacted a spiritual friend close to the family, and told her about the dream. She agreed it was significant and that I dreamt the dream to protect the person within the dream. We said a prayer for the person within the dream.

Trusting yourself is priceless. Not to be overly dramatic, but it can mean life or death. Trusting yourself is vitally important. As adults we are often brainwashed to do the opposite. In birth and sometimes death, we see clearly. There is no right or wrong time to decide to trust yourself. You will be where you need to be. Your intuition centered in love will always bring you home.

I've had prophetic dreams all my life. I developed the ability to see myself sleep, leave my body, and project myself. I am far from being the only one to experience this. Again, children are often sensitive to spiritual things and often see and hear things that adults don't see.

These children are spiritually gifted. All beings have this gift, whether they realize it or not. Your intuition is a gift. My spiritual intuitive muscle developed early on partly because of the trauma I experienced as a child through abuse from my mother's boyfriend. I learned to connect to supernatural energy, and it was a comfort to me. My intuition was my invisible safe place, and ultimately my intuition led me out of a ten-year cycle of abuse that started when I was five-years-old. My intuition gave me the strength to stand up for myself and trust that I could indeed set myself free. Perhaps your intuition is encouraging you to let go of a broken situation now. Listen to it, and you will be carried through.

The first fifteen years of my life consisted of a mixture of love, trauma, guilt, suffering, joy, wonderment, and more. My intuition led me through all of these changes. My intuition was here before I was taught man-made religion in my early years. Later on in my life, my intuition would take me deeper into the mysteries of true religion, which is not man-made. My intuition took me into the unknown and the unseen. My intuition has led me to experience all that I have experienced partly so that I can remind people to trust themselves. We need a constant reminder in a world that teaches that people don't really know what they want, and that people should "lean not unto their own understanding" (Proverbs 3:5), a grossly misunderstood scripture, that people incorrectly use-to manipulate others into not trusting themselves. People do know what they want. Your intuition can lead you and set your compass (Thibodeau, 2005). My intuition was here at birth, and your intuition was present too.

Going into my teenage years, I recall the challenge to trust myself developing as my involvement with Christianity grew, yet it took years and didn't start that way. I was "saved," at the age of fourteen and baptized at around sixteen-years-old. What appealed to me most about Christianity at the time was its affinity with divination, something often spoken of within the Bible, but condemned by Christians. I still felt safe within Christianity. I felt safe to experience and share my spiritual gifts of seeing and hearing. I used my intuition in everything that I did. In Christianity, I was called a prophet for the first time in 1994 by a woman who was like a mother to me. Her words would be repeated over and over by many people within the church world. These words meant to me that I was a vessel, and I only needed to express what needed and wanted to be expressed through words, dance, or demonstration. My exercises as a prophet strengthened my ability to hear and see the spirit world. This allowed me to put aside my ego and be willing to trust in the wisdom of my higher self.

I was a Christian virgin and determined to remain a virgin until marriage. At twenty-three, I married, and by twenty-five, I was divorced. By this time in my life, I had experienced a great deal of fine attunement within my intuition, which I still allowed to guide me, as I'd learned from birth. My Intuition led me into relationships and out of them. What I initially saw as a problem was, as my intuition taught me, the solution. My intuition allowed me to have these experiences for my own growth. My intuition has always managed to allow every situation to work out for my good. Your intuition is present within you at every phase of your life. I know there are times where it seems like you do not know what to do, yet if you are still enough, your higher self can guide you to the most necessary and loving course of action for the moment. There were many grounding exercises I've learned to help me tap into my intuition more effectively.

Your intuition will encourage you to go with the flow and step back into the unknown when you've wandered too far from your higher self. My time in Christianity ultimately led me deeper into myself and out of structured religion. I connected more closely to my dreams; I connected to my god self, beyond labeling. This was a journey of learning to trust my true self beyond what others thought. My intuition led me to various teachings, religions, businesses, places, and people, and ultimately to nothingness. By nothingness I mean stillness. My intuition has always led me right back to myself. Your intuition does the same. It leads you to you—the one that has been here since before you were born, the energic blueprint that leads and guides you.

Looking at my life in 2022, I can clearly see the importance of saying yes to yourself and no when your instincts tell you to say no. This is something I have learned to trust within myself over the years. It is one thing to hear and respond to our intuition; it is sometimes difficult, especially for women, to say no. Our intuition really is like a compass that tells us what our true North Star is. It helps us to fortify our boundaries. We are often in situations where we are learning how to trust ourselves within this classroom of life. As adults, we are finding our way back to what we naturally had as babies- to see, hear, and trust. We are relearning how to trust that the universe supports us and can bring us what we need in order to accomplish what it intuitively placed in us to accomplish. All living things know this. As humans, when life happens to us, we tend to doubt our intuition. We doubt that we've made the best decisions when we don't immediately encounter favorable outcomes.

We doubt ourselves when we experience a challenge or when things go wrong. Can you imagine what would happen if the bee gave up its natural intuition to pollinate flowers when it encountered a flower it couldn't pollinate? Should the bee not trust its intuition to pollinate flowers if it fails once, twice, even three times? No. Instead, the bee continues to trust its instincts, knowing it will be guided to flowers. You are guided and directed whether you realize it or not. Your intuition is attracting you or pulling you away. There is no right or wrong within what path you choose; yet what must be realized is that there are consequences for actions. These consequences are not good or bad; instead, they are consequences you may need for your growth.

You get to decide how attentive to your intuition you want to be. You can choose to have life keep sending you messages until you listen, or you can choose to cut your learning curve and take heed to what you know within your gut immediately. Either way, you are still progressing within this classroom of life. Learn to trust yourself, your intuition, and your experiences, that is the take home message of this chapter.

DR. BEE THOMAS

Dr. Bee Thomas is an NFT Artist, writer, and business educator. Her work was featured at San Diego's first NFT conference in April 2022. She was also a speaker at NFT NYC and featured in Times Square and LA NFT Expoverse. She is renowned for her published phenomenological groundbreaking research study on the Success Factors of African American Female Entrepreneurs and her achievements as a serial entrepreneur. Her Doctorate is in Business Administration.

Dr. Thomas has over two decades of experience teaching adult learners and creating academic-level curricula. She has taught at numerous colleges and has a licensing program for business owners.

Dr. Thomas is an author, NFT artist, speaker, and phenomenally successful African American Woman Business Owner. She is a professional business educator who teaches adult learners, an Air Force veteran, a former federal police officer, and a former college professor.

Dr. Thomas started her first company in 2007 and has been instrumental in consulting NFT artists, speaking on several stages about

Web3, and launching several businesses and brands. In addition to supporting, educating, and mentoring entrepreneurs at every chance she gets, she has also created numerous charities, helping women, children, and at-risk youth.

Connect with Dr. Thomas at https://www.drbeethomas.com/book.

CHAPTER 9

Relationships, Manipulations & Questions

Jacklyn Ryan

Intuition. Instinct. Gut Feeling. Something's off...

If only we follow this more often and act on it more quickly, where would you be?

I'll tell you where I'd be. A lot happier a lot earlier in my life and as strong in my 50s as I am becoming in my 60s!

We have all had to go through a myriad of assorted affairs and relationships to figure out the right mate. You always think, "Well, maybe this one will be IT, and so you try and work on the relationship for him to fit your needs. You readily want to fit his needs because He Might be The ONE. Reflecting, I wasted a lot of time on men who just couldn't cut it with me. Is that harsh? No, it's the fact. It takes two to tango unless you want to line dance! Make a list of what's really important to you and what you Need and what you Want in a life partner. In the first eight weeks of your new relationship, ask the questions and check the boxes.

I was riding four legged horses until high school, then I switched to chasing the two-legged asses. I smartened up later and returned to the four-legged horses! I gave my new beau a halter (the horses headgear) to put on my horse and lead him up to the barn. The halter was put on upside down and the underside strap was running down the horse's nose! I could never imagine how to put that on upside down! Well, he didn't know. Ok, but that was the beginning of a trying relationship for nine months. But, but, but... I met him at church!!

He began riding horses with me because I liked to, not because he liked to. He eventually became passive aggressive and needed more from me than I could give. I am very self-reliant and not a needy person, so I ended the relationship (which should've been earlier than later). I told him he was a good guy, but I just couldn't shoulder his insecurities. He was a "red flag" guy.

Next, I enjoyed skydiving once in a while. After returning to NW Arkansas, out of the "big cities," I tried Match.com for two weeks (that was Crazy!). My profile on Match.com profile read, "I like to scuba dive, skydive, and horseback ride." One guy I met owned a skydiving business and he was the pilot! I jumped out of his plane a few times and we enjoyed some good moments.

However, a few months into dating when I invited him to ride horses, he was a little hesitant and said horses don't like him. I got him on my trusted smaller red horse, Wind. While I was getting ready to get on my other larger horse, Wind ran away with him. You remember the song by Michael Martin Murphy, "Ride Like the Wind"? He finally got him stopped, got off, walked him back and said, "I told you horses don't like me!" Yeah, we broke up after that. I'm willing to jump out of airplanes, but he wouldn't ride my horse!

I relay these stories because we go through life trying to find the right partner. My husband, of twelve years now, is ideal. Still. We attended a charity event our first date. I wore my short black dress (you know the one) and had my hair done up. We had a grand time! Many people didn't know he was divorced and some knew me and couldn't believe we were together! He owned a clothing store in town, so definitely a city guy. Well, the next day I called and asked him to come out for a horse ride. I had my large black horse saddled up for him when he arrived.

Ladies, at my age, I've gotta qualify them fast! My paper roll of life was getting shorter past forty-five! Well, he enjoyed it! A week later, I took him for another ride. He enjoyed it! Actually, weeks later he confided in me that he thought he was going to die, but didn't say a word. Point is, this man had not ridden horses before, it became something he truly enjoyed, and not just because of me. We married ten months later. He had to ask me three times. I wanted to make sure he knew what he was asking! He still feeds the horses each morning!

So, relaying these brief relationship stories, I hope you will examine your relationship and use your intuition on how to navigate to the right mate. Or, just be happy and content with your awesome self!

Now, let's dive deeper into the abyss of intuition that led me down a sordid road.

I purposely uprooted my life and sold my house in Dallas, Texas, in 2003 to be closer to my aging parents. My stepmother passed in 2004, leaving my dad widowed. My mom had remained single after the divorce in 1971.

I was with dad and helped him when he had a quadruple bypass surgery in 2006. I helped on the farm any way I could. He had a "hired man," so at times there wasn't much I needed to do. He never got into a habit of calling me when he needed something. I always told him that I was just a phone call away.

He became busy dating and traveling while working on the farm. I proceeded to work real estate and figuring my way from leaving my home in Northwest Arkansas, lived in Dallas, Texas, Miami, Florida, returned to Dallas, then returned to back The Country, literally.

In 2014, dad fell and broke his hip. I could see his house from where I live. His close friend called me, so I rushed down and called 911. After his surgery, I was referred to a home care agency. They had a very nice woman who cared for him. A few months later, he fell and broke his other hip. My two brothers and I saw the need to increase his care to full time. It was very difficult to find a caregiver through the agency but, finally, after six weeks, Claire showed up. And that is the point! 1) She showed up, 2) on time 3) had a bright smile, and 4) was communicative and engaging! Dad liked her and we liked her. After a few weeks, I felt like I found a New Best Friend!

However, a few months later, I found a tire receipt for $900!? It was for her car! I alerted my family and we had a talk with dad and Claire. "It was just a loan! I was going to pay it back!," Claire said with tears streaming down her face. Dad was apologetic that they got "caught." Thereafter, reflecting, dad and Claire became more secretive.

We should've notified the agency and had her fired. But it was so difficult to find good, reliable help.

After two years passed, dad seemed a little distant to me. I eventually developed a suspicion, *but not soon enough*. I placed a recording device in his house. The first recording I heard between Dad and Claire:

"How's Jackie?" "She's a bitch," replied Claire. "Oh," Dad replied. "I need ink for my printer!" "I'll get you some," Dad replied.

That shook me. What? I thought we were on "good terms." Little did I know, she was working her way into his life and turning dad against me. I did more recordings for a while, but I had to quit because it was almost making me sick. I would work during the day, find a way to leave and pick up the recording device, listen for a few hours, and try to decipher the conversations amongst the old westerns on tv.

Another statement that rocked me to my core was when Claire said, "Nobody but me will care for you like I do!" There were many other statements; that's just a couple.

You may be wondering, "Why didn't she just confront Claire?" And that's what it would have been, a confrontation. Who would win? She would. She had dad wrapped around her finger. You can't argue with sex. As much as I didn't want to envision it, that was a strong possibility!

What I was learning through the recordings and from others, created within me a sense of burden about who is more guilty. Is it those who cause harm, or is it people like me who know and do not relay the information or do anything about it?

I eventually let my brothers know about the recordings. One advised me to stop and the other told Claire!? So, then Claire knew I was on to her. Big mistake. Don't ever let someone know you are on to them.

It's a long story, involving seven years of an unscrupulous, unethical, immoral caregiver, who threw two of the fellow caregivers "under the bus." How does one build themselves up by putting others down? She even let me know she had been in jail years earlier for meth. I let the agency know. Oh, of course they knew. Well, dad liked her!

Her employment continued until he died. The agency, in the seven years of caring for dad, averaged $210,000 per year from dad alone (that's a lot of money, $1.4 million). They put their business in front of what was best for dad.

There's an old saying that time is money. But when it comes to your integrity, time is actually more valuable than money. That's because you can always make more money, but once your integrity is gone, it's gone for good. So if you're ever tempted to put money above your integrity, just remember that in the long run, it's not worth it. You may be able to buy all the things you want in the short term, but without integrity, you'll never truly be happy. And what's the point of having a lot of money if you're not happy? So always keep your integrity intact – it's the most valuable thing you have.

People knew what was going on, but it was easier to turn a "blind eye" than to deal with it. Isn't that the way it goes nowadays?

Now, I'm going to delve into a broader spectrum. It's interesting to think about how people interacted with each other twenty years ago. It seems there was a lot more respect and understanding between people. Perhaps this was due to the fact that there weren't as many differing opinions. We would pick up the phone and talk. Now we use the phone for about everything except talking! Today, does it seem to you that the world is more Black or White? Right or Wrong? Good or Evil? Yes or No?

It doesn't really matter whether one accepts this or not; reality is not contingent on the popularity of belief.

A memorable moment for me was having dinner with a couple when the conversation branched into talking about the covid vaccine. The man shook his head and said, "I just can't believe why someone would not get the vaccine!" I remained silent while my husband piped up and said, "It's getting late; we should go." I found this moment quite humorous because it seemed like the man was more concerned about why people weren't getting the vaccine than he was about the actual virus.

I was recently involved in a real estate deal that required a Zoom® call with two other parties. I was caught off guard when, during the call, both parties began gleefully telling each other how happy they were to have received the jab. It was immediately clear that any questioning of the vaccine's efficacy would have been met with severe social disapproval. This made me realize just how prevalent social mind control has become.

I've known people who have been sick after getting the shot or have gotten covid a few times since receiving the shot, so I can understand why some people might be hesitant to get vaccinated. When people are afraid to express doubts or ask questions, it's a sign that groupthink is taking over. And that's never a good thing.

I propose we ask difficult questions. Yes, let's cross the line. Let's entertain doubt and uncertainty under your own initiative. Check your intuitiveness. When reading these questions, come from a place of curiosity and listen to your intuition rather than mainstream media or what others say is true. What does YOUR gut say?

➢ Are you sure medics have a sufficient understanding of health to advise you on novel diseases?

➢ Are you sure the mass media is principally journalism and not propaganda? (Watch the movie, read the book, *1984*, by George Orwell.)

➢ Are you sure the taxes you pay are wisely spent?

➢ Are you sure Joe Biden is the real and duly elected President with authority?

➢ Are you sure Donald Trump is the racist womanizer the media depicted him to be?

➢ Are you sure Barack Obama is the noble statesman the media promoted him as being?

➢ Are you sure Hillary Clinton is a genuine philanthropic fighter for women and the oppressed?

➢ Are you sure JFK was murdered by one lone gunman?

- ➢ Are you sure Jeffrey Epstein was only a child predator, or was he more?

- ➢ Are you sure you know how common it is for the famous or powerful to be blackmailed?

- ➢ Are you sure you know why the media is uninterested in Ghislaine Maxwell's client list?

- ➢ Are you sure our government works for us, the people who elected it and not a foreign power?

- ➢ Are you sure you understand how the American constitution could be subverted?

- ➢ Are you sure you would recognize a war of infiltration (by foreign powers) if one occurred?

- ➢ Are you sure our government agencies operate in our best interests?

- ➢ Are you sure there is an innate limit to the scale and scope of criminal enterprise?

- ➢ Are you sure there isn't a covert subtext or hidden agenda in most Hollywood movies?

- ➢ Are you sure tech companies like Google® and Facebook® are legitimate commercial operations?

- ➢ Are you sure your data is being handled lawfully and not divulged to criminals or governments?

- ➢ Are you sure you understand the role of secret societies and their true level of influence?

- ➢ Are you sure you have the understanding to spot use of unethical media mind control?

- ➢ Are you sure our history is accurately depicted in museums and as taught in school?

- ➢ Are you sure what is being taught in schools is fact and not opinions?
- ➢ Are you sure the rise of transgenderism and pedophilia is organic and unconcerning?
- ➢ Are you sure the Bible is just a collection of myths unrelated to modern society?
- ➢ Are you sure Neil Armstrong walked on the moon?
- ➢ Are you sure the infrastructure you see above ground is where the action is?
- ➢ Are you sure certain politicians and celebrities are not professionally masked? (Google® Jonna Mendez)
- ➢ Are you sure Trayvon Martin, George Floyd, and many others are any more special than all the others who have been murdered?
- ➢ Are you sure you would know if a cult took over society and cult membership was "normal"?
- ➢ Are you sure the powerful would teach you the thinking tools needed to spot their power?
- ➢ Are you sure it's safe to form an opinion away from the media without checking sources yourself?
- ➢ Are you sure the government told the whole truth about September 11th, 2001? (How does glass and metal fall into a heap of rubble and other buildings collapse later?)
- ➢ Are you sure you have grasped the extent and significance of human trafficking in society?
- ➢ Are you sure that a new genocide would appear in an instantly recognizable form?

➢ Are you sure you understand the power of the Vatican, City of London, and Washington, DC, as forms of micro-state with global reach?

➢ Are you sure that any science or technology that conferred great power would automatically be used for the benefit of humanity rather than hoarded or subverted?

➢ Are you sure that you have set boundaries about what evil is capable of and your own vulnerability to deception?

➢ Are you sure you know what/who others worship, and have you aligned yourself to their deities?

➢ Are you sure what the media calls "QAnon" exists as described, without having looked yourself?

➢ Are you sure you know the extent to which your institutions are fraudulent or hijacked?

➢ Are you sure all "conspiracy theorists" are crazy?

Are you sure?

Really?

Check your intuition.

JACKLYN (JACCI) RYAN

Jacklyn (Jacci) Ryan's bestselling book, *CareGivers ScareTakers: Exposing Fraud in Senior Care*, is making waves. This riveting memoir blows the lid off of the senior care system.

With an aging population, families are struggling with dependable, trusted care. This process is riddled with problems. What can we do to protect our parents from abuse and financial theft from unscrupulous caregivers?

Jacklyn Ryan is a professional just like you. When a crisis happened, she instantly faced that heart-wrenching time in life when her parents were no longer able to care for themselves. Reaching out for help and trusting home care agencies, she soon discovered that appearances can be deceiving. In the trenches of caregiver nightmares, Jacklyn has learned the pitfalls and landmines of inappropriate and unscrupulous "ScareTakers." With powerful personal stories, and extensive research on this undeniable problem, Jacklyn is armed with life-changing information that can revise the process for those looking for appropriate and trustworthy care for their loved ones. Jacklyn is a Senior Care Advocate, consultant and speaker.

Jacklyn is a USA Today and Wall Street Journal bestselling author featured in the anthology book *Success Mindsets: How Top Entrepreneurs Succeed in Business and Life* published by Leaders Press.

Topics:

Hiring a Caregiver - What You Need to Know BEFORE You Make That Decision.

Tools for checking out agencies and caregivers, finding reviews and learning how to research references.

Don't wait for a Crisis to happen! Prepare YOUR OWN Care Ahead of Time. We plan for many life events, but neglect to make a plan for how or where we're going to live when we can no longer live on our own. Make Your Plan and Put it in Writing.

Raising the Bar on Caregivers will Raise the Bar on the Quality of Care.

Connect with Jacci at https://caregiverscaretakers.com.

CHAPTER 10

Wounded Healer

Kathi Sohn

Choice is to the soul what water is to the body. It can nourish and cleanse us and there is no life without it. We all constantly choose what to think, say, do, and believe, sometimes from our conscious mind and too often from the unconscious, habit mind. If I were to pull the thread back to the initial choice that helped make me who I am today, I would find myself back to the time of my first breath in this world.

My life began in 1961 as an emergency when my distraught birth mother caused my severely premature birth at the end of her second trimester. All one point eight pounds of my tiny body chose, in that incubator, to survive – no, to *thrive*, despite what had happened to me. There were some negative effects from my long time in the incubator, and they were ultimately a blessing. It was through healing my own trauma that I found my life's mission to share an amazing healing method with the world.

When I was about seven years old, I remember being in the doctor's office, frozen in terror as the white lab coat-clad man sat in his chair waiting for my answer to his question. I just stared at him until my mother broke the silence to respond. The doctor snapped his gaze to her and said, "Ma'am, I asked your *daughter* the question!" "But she's not answering you!," my mother replied in exasperation.

After that day, I became comfortable talking one-on-one to individuals but speaking in front of a group gave me that same feeling of terror I felt in the doctor's office. I know that public speaking is a common fear, but this was gripping dread of just announcing my name! As soon as I knew it was going to be my turn to talk, I would get a huge rush of adrenalin and my heart would start pounding. Once I felt all the attention on me, I would nearly pass out from the overwhelming fear.

My audience evolved from fellow students to employees when I became a manager and needed to lead staff meetings. The anxiety I felt was compounded by not wanting to appear nervous in front of my employees. My anxiety lessened a bit once I joined Toastmasters to get practice speaking in front of a supportive, familiar group. The problem ultimately persisted, and I would often get bright red blotches on my face and neck when I was in front of a group that I found intimidating.

Then one day, I discovered that my attention anxiety was rooted in the trauma of my earliest days as a rejected, extremely premature baby in intensive care. I was peered at very often in my incubator by the medical staff, some either thinking or saying aloud that they didn't believe I would make it. My body might have been tiny and frail, but it indeed recorded in body memory, *they watch me to see when I'm going to die.* I'm certain this was also the reason the doctor in the white lab coat frightened me. Being the center of attention in a public speaking scenario would key this up, because being critically watched first occurred for me in a life and death situation. A powerful new healing method helped me discover the root cause of my extreme fear and then taught me how to free myself from it. The result was complete relief from the gripping anxiety and now public speaking is an easy and very fulfilling part of my work.

In the years before I discovered the root cause of my social anxiety, I became increasingly withdrawn. I was 33 years old with a string of failed relationships, partly because I was afraid of commitment. My adoptive mother was very loving and was also extremely protective and emotionally enmeshed with me. She never thought any of my boyfriends were good enough and I came to value her opinion over my own, sabotaging relationship after relationship.

One day I finally surrendered to letting God be in control of relationships in my life. I could feel the shift in my body when I finally admitted I was lost and lonely. I had always been very spiritual and willing to let God oversee *almost* everything in my life. I guess I figured my mother was in charge of my relationships, so God didn't need to be!

About six months after this shift, I met David William Sohn, who I would learn was the creator of an amazing healing method called the Body Memory Process. He was brought to my doorstep on the 4th of July in 1994 by some friends, one of whom had said to me for months, "You've really got to meet this guy! You're perfect for each other!" David had also been encouraged to meet "this girl" in the same way and now it finally happened. You might be wondering if my mother liked David. She didn't. However, I finally found the courage to tell her that he was the one and I was not going to change my mind. My choice to surrender to a higher power and to trust my intuition finally brought me my soulmate and in May of 1997 we were married.

Not long after David came into my life, I learned that I had been adopted. I was in my thirties and had no idea until I was talking to my brother on the phone one day. I was shocked, yet suddenly a lot of things made sense. My adoptive mother had told me I was born prematurely, but that is all I remember as significant regarding my birth. It wasn't until after David and I were married that I finally brought up this emotionally charged subject with my mother. Whenever I would go home to visit, it never seemed like the right time to bring it up and, honestly, I was worried about what Mom's reaction to my questions would be.

One particularly beautiful day I was home on a weekend visit with my parents without David. I was out on a walk that Saturday when I got a sudden, powerful urge to talk to Mom about my adoption. I can't explain why I was filled with such courage. I just knew the right time had come to get everything out in the open and I could hardly wait to get home.

When we talked, my mother teared up and told me the story of how she and my father had been unable to have children of their own after trying for about ten years. They decided to adopt and sought to give a loving home to children who had been deeply traumatized at the beginning of their lives. Mom told me she didn't know a lot about my birth mother, but she was aware that she had attempted a home abortion at about six months gestation.

My mother said that when my two brothers and I each reached the age of seven she had us read a book entitled, *The Chosen Baby*. I remembered the book and that I loved to read it over and over. Thinking back, I don't ever remember realizing that it was about me! My mother said she had agonized over the right time to tell me (again) that I was adopted after I said something when I was about thirteen that made her realize I didn't know. As she sat there, tears of guilt streaming down her face, I shared with her that I, too, had agonized over when to bring up the subject once I had the discussion with my brother. I told her that I understood completely what she had gone through and that it made me love her and Dad even more.

Within about a year of this discussion, my mother learned she had progressed breast cancer and she passed away quickly after her surgery because the cancer had metastasized. She elected to not have chemotherapy or radiation and was gone within ten months of her diagnosis.

By this time, I had learned a lot about the Body Memory Process and had done the work on myself to heal my social anxiety. When David and I met, he was beginning to write a book on the work, at the encouragement of many of his clients. Over the next few years, David would write during the day, and I would edit when I came home from my job with the Department of Defense. I gained a deep understanding of the work and saw how it helped clients to heal diseases, improve relationships, and become open to more prosperity in their lives because they discovered and then released deeply entrenched ideas about themselves that weren't true. In 2004, *Escaping the Labyrinth* was published to explain a powerful way to set people free from their past.

Up until about the age of seven, children create core beliefs about themselves, others, and the world. The problem is they are still very immature, the others around them are but a handful of caregivers and family, and their world is extremely small. Children are very egocentric and not yet logical, so it is easy for them to draw these conclusions based on highly emotional and often traumatic events. Even highly emotional *positive* events can create a belief. Consider a scenario of a three-year-old girl sitting on her daddy's knee. She loves her daddy's attention, which is sometimes hard to get, and he suddenly leans in close and says lovingly, "You'll always be my little girl!" She might file this away as "I'll always be your little girl," which seems innocuous for the child. Then when she grows up and suddenly starts acting like a little girl in the presence of a powerful male, such as her boss, difficulties can ensue. Research has proven that babies in the womb are intelligent and can form beliefs while still in utero. This happens as well at birth and during the formative years.

When David was fourteen years old, he had a near death experience during a struggle with double staph pneumonia. Following his recovery, he was told by doctors he would never be truly well because of the effect of the disease on his lungs. David railed against this, and after college began a quest to discover all available ideas related to a level of wellness that was more than merely the absence of disease. David created the Body Memory Process based on the mind-body connection, the intelligence of babies in the womb, the fact that children form core beliefs before the age of seven, and the power of beliefs to create our reality. David called these core beliefs "vows" because, like wedding vows, they make a powerful statement to live by.

For the 25 years that David and I were together, I continued to use the work to discover and heal other decisions I had made in my early life. I found that I had vows like "everything is my fault" and "I have to take care of myself."

In October 2019, David passed away and I found myself suddenly a widow and a single mom. In 2009, David and I had a son, Benjamin, who is on the autism spectrum, and we had Sarah in 2013. The family and I were in Hawaii for what was to be my last assignment with the Department of Defense before I retired, when David became ill and went quickly downhill.

I knew I couldn't break down and give up. I needed to gather all my strength and take action to support two grieving children. While quickly planning retirement for the end of the school year and navigating a global pandemic to sell my property in Hawaii, I was buying a home in Alabama before setting foot in it.

One day in early 2021, I looked up and realized we were well-settled in our new home, new school, and new town. After working full time for 36 years, what was I to do with my newly found time? It didn't take long for me to decide to pick up the torch called the Body Memory Process and ensure that my late husband's life's work didn't fade away.

During the first year, I focused on establishing an online presence and refining a course that David and I had previously begun putting together. My plan was to promote the work by having a website and dipping my toe into the social media advertising world to let people know the course was available. I thought that I could just sit behind the scenes and let the Internet do the job for me. By the end of the year, I was not satisfied with my results and turned inward for guidance on how to move forward.

What came from my meditation was a realization that this work is transformative and that it is greatly needed by many people everywhere who had been suffering from trauma even before the pandemic hit. I knew that playing small was not the answer and decided at that point to begin doing what I would have thought to be impossible before experiencing the Body Memory Process. I made the choice to begin speaking on podcasts, on webinars, in homemade videos and in front of live audiences to spread the word about the work. I was no longer dipping in my toe – *I made the choice to be all in!* I have since mused that when I was working for the Department of Defense I wasn't allowed to talk to the media. I was finally able to step out into the light and embrace talking to the public.

It is not a coincidence that I experienced such a high dose of trauma in the womb and at birth, to then grow up and discover my life's mission to help others free themselves of the long-term impact of early life trauma. David used to say that people with difficult beginnings can become a "wounded healer" because their capacity to heal can be magnified by their own healing journey.

I continue to make choices to shape the world I want for myself and my children and many of them are choices to forgive. I have forgiven David for leaving me to raise our young children alone, knowing he is always by my side. I have forgiven my birth mother because she did the best that she could with what she had at the time. She gave me tremendous gifts of strength and tenacity that have served me well through the years and will continue to do so. I have also forgiven my adoptive mother and thank her for teaching me the importance of trusting my own intuition, finding my own voice, and not being afraid to tell what I know to be truth.

MS. KATHI SOHN

Ms. Kathi Sohn retired in 2020 from a 36-year Department of Defense career, which included work in Bosnia, Iraq, and Afghanistan. She began her career with four years in the U.S. Army. Ms. Sohn graduated with the highest distinction and a prestigious award from the Naval War College Master's Program and holds a Masters in Conflict Analysis and Resolution from George Mason University.

After the 2019 death of her beloved husband, David William Sohn, she decided to dedicate her time to her two young children and to promoting the powerful healing work created by David, called the Body Memory Process. For over 30 years, this work has created positive changes for clients facing health, relationship, and prosperity issues. The Body Memory Process facilitates the discovery and release of limiting and sometimes destructive core beliefs created at birth and in early childhood. Ms. Sohn created a multi-media course, "Discover Your Childhood Vows, Change Your Life," and is currently writing a book on the Body Memory Process.

Connect with Kathi at https://bodymemoryprocess.com.

CHAPTER 11

Trust Your Intuition to Reach Your Life Dreams!

Linley Baker

In high school, I took the usual career insights test, which was graded by a computer. It told me I should be a college math professor. But I knew as I read the results that *they were wrong.*

I loved math, but I was not interested in endless research and "17th-dimensional" math problems. If I were to work with math, I wanted a more practical use of it, solving real-life problems.

Computers are great at many things, but one of them is NOT intuition. It could understand our abilities and aptitudes, but it could not understand our feelings and ideas about them.

I was particularly introspective as a junior in high school, knowing I would soon need to choose a college and a focus or major that would affect my whole future life.

I focused on my three "life dreams." My three **M**'s. I knew I wanted to be a **M**athematician, a **M**usician, and a **M**other. My intuition told me these would make me happy. I have used these as guiding stars and figured out how to live out these dreams as the years have gone by.

The first **M**–**M**ath–was my favorite subject in school. I was always ahead and even competed on the Mathlete team at high school. Yes– math for fun!

Music was a huge part of my life. I started piano lessons at age 4, taught by my grandmother, and viola at age 10, taught by my mother. I performed in choirs and orchestras, and as a soloist in high school.

My last **M**–**M**otherhood–would wait, so it was time to decide if it would be Math or Music for college. My intuition told me I would like either, but I had to choose a primary one.

I finally thought, "I don't know what my future will be, so it would be better to study something which would lead to a job that has a high chance of supporting myself." Math has more jobs, so I chose that over music.

M–Math

My father became aware of a type of mathematician, called actuar- ies, through his work for an insurance company. He introduced this career to me thus, "If you want to work with math, apply it to some- thing practical, and not be discriminated against, be an actuary." I was intrigued.

It was a practical application of mathematics! My dad said that people didn't care whether you were male or female, just whether you could do the complex calculations. So I studied actuarial math and business at the Wharton School, and started on the long series of ex- ams for certification.

After college graduation, I landed a job as an actuary for Nation- wide Insurance in Columbus, Ohio. I loved tackling complex mathe- matical problems. I solved them not just for workable numbers, but also used my creativity for great business solutions.

M–Motherhood

I met my future husband there in Ohio, and we married when I was 21 years old. In a couple years, we had our first of six children, a son. Motherhood!

I always knew I wanted to raise my children, myself. I wanted them to learn morals, religion, reading, to love learning, and music.

I wanted to raise my children *more* than I wanted my career. This is how I wanted to live Motherhood. So I was willing to risk *not* making my career goal. I knew I was limiting my number of working years, and even risking not returning…. I thought that if I had my children while I was young, I might still have career time left after they grew up.

So at the end of maternity leave after my second son was born, I resigned my beloved position with Nationwide Insurance. That was really hard. It was the only time in my adult life that I stuttered: "I want to T-t-t-terminate my position…" I trusted my intuition that I would be happier in spite of the sadness of leaving my job.

I also hoped that I could eventually resume my career, but not until my children grew up. Everyone said that it wasn't possible. To leave for a couple of years and come back *was* possible, though it might be hard. Many people have done that. To leave for a generation—impossible.

I decided that I wanted to *make* it possible. I wanted **Motherhood** *and* my **Math** career so much that I decided to try to do both. Maybe it wasn't impossible…

George Bernard Shaw stated, *"You see things that are and say, 'Why?' But I dream things that never were and say, 'Why not?'"*

M–Music

When my youngest child entered first grade, I started to have some time to myself. I wasn't ready to return to full-time work. I had six children ages 6 to 16, and that was a lot more than full-time work! But there was some discretionary time during the day when the children were at school.

I was also thinking about my obituary. I wanted to be sure it said something about music. I figured that if I got a degree in music, my family would remember to include music in my obit.

Rather than working on a bucket list of cool things to do, I focus on who I want to *become*. And I hope that will be reflected in my obituary. My intuition told me that music would help me feel happy and fulfilled.

So, at age 39, I auditioned for a master's degree in viola performance at a local university. I was accepted and dove in. I loved making and studying great music with other adults!

I was surprised by the effect on me from studying music. I found my capacities *increased*! I was happier and more fulfilled. I was able to *better* serve my family because I spent part of each day fulfilling my passion, my dream in Music. I was so happy to fulfill my third M dream in Music.

Hoping to Return

Even though everyone told me that it was impossible to get back to professional work after such a long break, I was hoping for it anyway. My intuition told me it was worth a try.

Henry Ford wisely stated, *"If you think you can or if you think you can't, you're right."*

Hope. I found opportunities to teach actuarial science and math, and to volunteer in Actuarial Education. Hope gave me the power to fit them into my already busy life–raising six children. Hope *is* power.

Would it work? Would I be able to return to my beloved career?

Zig Ziglar quipped, *"Those who say it can't be done are usually interrupted by others doing it."*

Trying to Return

After 19 years, I was ready to return to corporate work, but six months of job searching yielded nothing. Everyone wanted recent experience. I screamed in my mind, "How can I get recent experience if no one will hire me??????"

Finally, I found a company that was willing to interview me, not for my actuarial abilities, but because they were looking for an actuary who spoke English, an Asian language, and a European language. I knew English, Japanese, and French, from living overseas and trying to make friends, so they were willing to interview me.

In the interview, we talked about what I had done to keep up, often for little or no money, over the past two decades. They were impressed and decided to give me a chance. I was so excited!

As Ralph Waldo Emerson said, *"The future belongs to those who prepare for it."*

Return to Work

Now it was time to see: Could I actually do the job I had left almost two decades before?

I was excited but nervous to resume corporate work!

But I also had 19 years of catching up to do regarding the day-to-day work. All the software and hardware had changed.

I found that I had a lot of questions, stupid questions. Things I thought I would not have to ask if I had been to college in the past five years, in almost any major! To live with myself, I had to set a limit: I could ask a particular stupid question only once. So I documented the answer and made sure I understood it.

Then only seven months into my job, I was promoted to manager. How did that happen? It turned out that all the organizational and leadership skills I developed in the family and the community prepared me for business leadership as well!

Virtual Antennas

I learned that the key is to keep all your life dreams in your vision, even if something is not currently an active part of your life. Erect one virtual antenna for each dream. This sets you up to jump on opportunities that may fit with a dream that is not currently your focus.

If I had not been thinking about my actuarial career when I was a full-time mother, I may have missed the opportunities I had to work part time in math, and then have missed the opportunity to resume my career. If I had not been thinking about music, I might not have gone back to school for it.

Balancing Goals Through Life

You can have the career you want and reach your personal goals, too. Just maybe not everything all at once.

Take time to be self-reflective and decide what major things you want to do with your life. What might you *really* regret near the end of your life, if you never did it? What makes you happy? What dream did you give up long ago? These ideas are usually not random or spurious–they are your intuition giving you direction for your life.

For me with three dreams, they were always there, but the priority of each changed with each season of life. I always had my antenna up for music and math opportunities. Even if it is just a background thought-process, you're still connected to your dream.

Fear

Often people are afraid to try something new, even if they think they will like it, out of fear of failure. Things are usually not as scary as they might feel at first. I think it is important to replace feelings with thinking—to assess <u>what would be the worst consequence</u> of your efforts not working out, or of realizing it wasn't what you wanted after all.

I had to overcome a lot of fear to return to actuarial work!

If your intuition is telling you you like something, listen to it! You will probably find something you love. It's not about *not* being afraid. It is about not being *too* afraid to do what you *really* want to do.

When Life Knocks You Down

In May of 2019, my husband of 35 years suddenly left me and our whole life together. He quit our church that we had been so dedicated to. He quit our gym (so I got all his unpaid personal training–haha!).

Most of all, I couldn't comprehend–at first–that he was leaving me. We had gotten married in a ceremony that was forever, not just "until death do you part." And we had had a great marriage–great companionship, six children, lived internationally, made music as a family, and enjoyed lots of great conversations about ideas and how to live our lives.

Major shock!

I accepted his choice to live as he wanted. I tried to embrace single life. I enjoyed directing the choir at church, joined a symphony orchestra, and got a cute, female Havanese puppy for companionship. I went on a new-single trip by myself to Hawaii in October, just days after the divorce was final, and was just starting to catch my balance on the carpet of single life.

Then at the end of that month, my boss told me that she was laying me off. This was another great shock. Now, as a single person, I could not rely on my spouse's income while I searched for a new position (as I had done several times for my husband). With my world upside down, I felt that carpet of single life ripped out from under me and I was flailing.

2020 Will be Better

It was such a bad year, I just wanted it to be over. So I started getting excited to have a new year. I told people I knew 2020 would be better than 2019! I was sure of it. I had no husband to lose and no job to lose, so it couldn't be worse! And…while 2020 was a terrible year for most people, it was better than 2019 for me!

When you have no income and no other means of support, you have to move where there is no mortgage or rental fee. As part of my divorce settlement, I received a home in Utah, debt-free. At first, I was really depressed about having to move there, but a good friend remarked what a blessing it was to have a home available, and I realized I really needed to be thankful.

I tried to look at the bright side and decided that the loss of my husband and job was a gift of time to write my book that I had been planning for a long time: *Don't Be Afraid to Do What You Really Want to Do–Reach All Your Life Dreams.*

I had been wronged, but decided to embrace change rather than fight for recompense. It freed me up to move forward.

I set a goal to NOT think about my divorce ALL THE TIME. At some future point. I wasn't ready right then, but my intuition told me I wanted to get there.

I studied how to do that. I learned that the best way was to have something new to think about. Writing my book turned out to be my solution. As I thought about *how* and *what* to write, that finally released my brain from constantly figuring out my new identity.

Betrayed, Not Trashed

Major challenges often come with new labels, ones we might not like. Divorcée, widow, cripple, cancer-survivor, and so on. But I was <u>betrayed</u>, *not trashed*! People betrayed probably have new problems, but their worth cannot change.

"Divorcée" is not my core identity. I am a good, beautiful human, a child of God of infinite worth. Nothing that anyone does to me can change that!

We must not let such labels take over our identity. Our most important names or labels reflect our core goodness and worth. Our intuition tells us who we really are. We must trust in it to preserve our self-worth.

I'm glad I trusted my intuition. As I reached my dreams in the 3 M's, I experienced joy and fulfillment. And it helped me see myself as I really am, in the hard times.

What about you?

What are your life dreams? Trust your intuition about what you would really like to do! It will guide you to happiness, fulfillment, and confidence, and your true self.

LINLEY BAKER

Linley Baker grew up in Massachusetts, about 60 miles from where her Hopkins ancestors landed on the Mayflower in 1620. After graduating with high honors from the Wharton School of Business of the University of Pennsylvania, Linley pursued a successful actuarial career (applied mathematics) in insurance. She earned Fellowship in the Society of Actuaries (like a Ph.D. in applied math) at age 25.

After becoming a mother, Linley quit corporate work to raise her children, eventually numbering six, in 4 countries: Japan, China, France, and the United States. She is multilingual in Japanese, French, and Spanish.

She earned a Master of Music Viola Performance degree from Ball State University while the children were home. Linley returned to her profession in 2012 and in only five years she was promoted to full vice president. Linley shares that unconventional career paths are possible—and sometimes better—through her company Linfluence, LLC.

Her first book is for everyone: *Don't Be Afraid to Do What You Really Want to Do – Reach All Your Life Dreams,* and is available on Amazon. She has a related keynote speech—Reaching Your Life Dreams. Her second book is currently in process: *Betrayed, Not Trashed.* It is about how to deal with trials like divorce and keep up your self-worth. She already presents a related speech, Finding Grace in Trials, which is a speech hyphenated by classical music that she performs. Linley currently lives in Salt Lake City, Utah, with Puccini, her Havanese puppy, and works as an actuary, speaker, and math tutor.

Connect with Linley at www.linfluence.pro.

CHAPTER 12

A Transcendent Traveler
"From My Heart to My Hands"

Nicole Mendes

A little over a week ago, I began each morning drinking and having cacao rituals, subconsciously being called to open and prepare my heart for this moment of writing. A ceremony that I blessedly discovered during my travels to Costa Rica. A ceremony and ritual that is unfamiliar to most of those living here in the States. When most Americans and westerners hear the word cacao, immediate thoughts of overly sweet chocolate and desserts infiltrate their minds. Completely disconnected to the plant, the fruit itself and the process that, once it's fermented, roasted and turned into a rich delicious cup of cacao, is a true ancestral form of heart opening medicine. Each day this past week, after having my cacao, I could feel the beginning of expansion and preparation for this moment. Now on this gorgeous and oddly warm November day, I sit here on the outside back patio of the Palace of Pleasures, a magical space where I have most recently landed. Even more importantly, this is where I most recently expanded. I'm thinking to myself, the thyme is here and it is now. It is now that I am ready to fully transcend upon many years of hiding, fear and repression and turn them into years of expansion and expression.

Although, if I am going to be honest, I've been struggling and spending countless hours thinking about how I am going to approach writing this chapter. Having lived what feels like multiple lifetimes in the past 27 years of my life, it's been quite challenging to think of a starting point. With many stories, layers of trauma and healing that I've undergone, it almost seems impossible to condense it into one chapter. However, with every sip of cacao, my heart begins to open more and more. Reminding myself to tune in and breathe deep into the depths of my heart, and to realize that this right here, this rawness, this natural flow as I write, truly letting my heart speak to my hands, this is exactly how it is supposed to happen. It is almost like when I am gifted with a bounty of fresh farm produce in the kitchen, with my years of experience as a chef I immediately and, without any second-guessing, can take these ingredients and transform them into something delicious.

Now with an open heart and letting go of the second-guessing, it's time for me to once again face fear in its eyes, to follow that intuition, that internal knowing. However, this time, it won't be as the chef I am, but as the transgender woman that I am, the woman that I have always been, the one who has been there all along, right from the beginning of my life, guiding me to this very moment of transformation. This is the moment to open my voice to the world to create a new type of delicious content, taking the words of my heart and putting them into words on paper. I am hopeful that my words, emotions, and stories will help others to transcend and keep moving forward in their journey as I continue moving forward and expanding in mine.

For most of my life I have felt like an outsider, like I don't really belong anywhere. Constantly, I struggled to navigate my femininity, finding my place, finding my voice and fitting in as a woman in the world. For the longest time, I have been carrying a lot of shame surrounding my transgender identity. Subconsciously and willingly hiding it. Terrified to express it. Still walking through life like I am carrying this deep dark secret that can fall out from under me at any moment. Creating a level of unhealthy anxiety, deep inside I was questioning, will I ever be "woman" enough? Ultimately I was stuck in a phase lacking love and self-acceptance for this part of me. Flowing through life, trying to block out this truth of who I am, is not a healthy way to live. I never expected that life post-surgery, I would still be facing all of these insecurities and emotions. At the time, some naive part of me assumed that once I got my vagina all of these things would just simply fade away. Well that's the beauty of life, constantly keeping you on edge so you can keep on growing. This act alone of writing is liberating this part of myself; is a transformation and affirmation, in and of itself.

This past year for me has truly been one of shedding off layers. It's quite amazing to reflect on how I have arrived at this moment. It wasn't until recently that a great deep shift occurred. An unexpected shift that I didn't see coming, but one I have only longed for. I was guided to a festival called Unifier in Western MA, guided there by an incredible Anjel (intentional misspelling). I had never heard of the Unifier festival before, but once I found out what it was about and was offered the chance to go, that internal voice I've been tuning into more and more compelled me to go. Not really knowing what to expect I surrendered to the flow. It was a gorgeous August day, the warmth of the sun beaming down into the forest reflecting off the trees and the beautiful pond nearby. The energy in the air was similar to the Solstice festival experienced in Guatemala, a space that invited everyone to come as they are. I spent a decent amount of time wandering around and wondering why I was truly here. Oftentimes in these types of spaces my introverted side kicks in and takes hold. When I found out there was a red tent, which is a safe space and container that is held and hosted by and for women, I felt called to enter the space. Hesitating at first, I put it off for a while.

It wasn't until later that evening that a ceremony was happening. Unaware of the details, I finally gained the courage to enter. Upon entering my body filled with intimidation, that outsider feeling followed me into the tent. Having no idea of the depths of the journey I was about to embark on, I found a little space to make myself comfortable and lay down. There were two lovely women holding and creating the container, leading us on a drumming meditation. It started quite calmly with a very subtle and gentle beat guiding us, allowing us to gracefully enter into our hearts and souls. We were guided to go to an internal space, a space that was familiar, yet foreign in many ways. As the drumming intensified so did the clarity of my vision. After flashes of water, sights of the ocean, I had arrived at an impressive Oak Tree among an expansive forest. The tree symbolic of a womb, I was asked to enter with the intention to receive a gift, a gift from my inner maiden. She was there to show us something to help us receive a part of ourselves that needed to be reclaimed. When confronted with the task to face her and to ask for the gift, things became blurry for me. At this point the drumming had multiplied in intensity. The harder I tried to hone in to focus and face my inner maiden it was as if only flashes of her would swiftly come and go. Being unable to fully see her filled me with a deep sense of curiosity, and ultimately a question of why, why can't I see her, why can't I face her? What is blocking me? As the drumming died down, I could feel the space I entered beginning to fade away and began slowly coming out of the vision. Taking several moments to let what was just experienced settle within me, feeling slightly perplexed, yet letting the questions sit within me.

Afterwards, while the container was still being beautifully held, each of us was allowed, if comfortable enough, to share what we experienced. After hearing each woman share parts of their journey and vivid descriptions of their inner maidens, the questions that came up for me only settled deeper. What was it that was truly blocking me from seeing that part of myself, what is the gift here to be received? Why is it that they all had vivid descriptions of their maidens and I didn't. A bit nervous I decided to describe what came up for me and how I was struggling to see my inner maiden. As I was describing this, I realized what the blocks were and that I am honestly only at the beginning of discovering her and tapping into this feminine energy that I hold within. I've spent more than half my life living and conforming to an identity that was so far removed from who I am, so no wonder why it was hard for me to see her. It felt good to share, however I could feel something else brewing inside, something that has been building up for the past fifteen years, back to very first time I discovered the word transgender and realized that I was destined to embody my life as a woman.

As the space continued to evolve, some shared chants and songs. One girl started singing a simply beautiful and affirming chant that went like:

"I Am Woman,

I Am Beautiful,

I Am Woman,

I Am Free."

As simple as it was, I closed my eyes and chanted along. Letting each word sink inside me. Huge vibrations, and waves of energy filled me as these words left my mouth, activating my throat chakra, I felt a sense of groundedness. For a brief moment I opened my eyes, scanned the room, and as I sang these words, felt deep, deep affirmation and resonation, that here. I am, in this sacred red tent, among all these women, for once feeling that I too, "I Am Woman, I Am Beautiful, I Am Free."

Waves of emotions were crashing into me. An invitation to make offerings and releases at an altar was offered and the space continued to be held. A few of the women went up and made their offerings, releases and shed their own layers. Each of us supporting one another and creating sisterhood. Feeling compelled, sitting there with these lyrics still lingering inside me, a strong energy grasped a hold of me, moved me, to right in front of the altar, in front of all the women. With a subtle shake, and pulsating nerves I knew what I had to do. Not knowing how it would leave me, I began to speak:

"Umm, hi everyone, I have never really done this before."

Nervously speaking.

"I'm not typically the type to speak in front of people, but a huge energy got hold of me...... and here...... here I am. It's long overdue. I need to release something...... something so deep, something that I've been holding onto for far, far too long. And it is time, it is time to, to let it go."

Completely terrified, but completely alive, with an outer-body experience the words just left me and kept leaving me.

"I am Trans, a Transwoman, and I am beautiful, and I am WOMAN! And I am so scared, scared to show the world this part of me. Because I don't have a womb, because I don't menstruate, because I can't birth, I feel so different, like I'm not complete. But right here and right now in front of all you magical women, I am feeling so complete and so affirmed for once in my life. Riding these lyrics I Am Woman and I am beautiful."

"It doesn't serve me any more to let these insecurities take hold of me. I am here to find my inner goddess to tune in and discover my maiden, because I know how beautiful she is and can be."

For a sudden moment, as I made this release, a wave of stillness arrived. A flash of 17-year-old me handcuffed in a police car, became present. Seventeen-year-old Nicole who had just witnessed her friend beaten unconscious by the police. The seventeen-year-old Nicole, who had also been thrown and head hit into the ground, searched for drugs. The seventeen-year-old Nicole or as I used to be called Nick, who was so lost in a world of selling drugs and getting high, had spoken to me.

She said, "Thank you... Thank you for never giving up. Thank you for continuing to fight every damn day to get to this moment. Thank you, thank you for overcoming what seemed like a slither of a dream. I knew you could do it. I knew you would transcend."

What felt like a lifetime, had passed in just a matter of minutes. Tears and trembling left my body, flushed out from deep within, finally released. As I was sitting there feeling many emotions, one woman chimed in and made an invitation for all the women in the tent. Not remembering her name, but never forgetting her, she said, "I'd like to invite all of you to make a chant and intention for Nicole, after me if we could all say in our most beautiful voices, Nicole is Goddess." In three very beautiful waves, all the women in the tent chimed in and chanted.

"Nicole is Goddess,

Nicole is Goddess,

Nicole is Goddess."

The sensation I was feeling, of receiving and letting these simple but powerful words land into my heart space is hard to put words to. Years of insecurity, doubt, shame, and hiding were washed away from me. Feelings of affirmation, wholeness and relief were the new energetic waves crashing into me.

I left that night feeling lighter.

Now as I sit here writing this story, it's just a continuation of the release I made that night. I am filled with a sense of gratitude, that despite all the challenges and dark moments I wouldn't trade this journey for anything. Finally feeling blessed for this transgender identity, to have lived life on both sides and all the way in between. Realizing that maybe one of the purposes that life has for me is to help inspire others regardless of gender, orientation or ethnicity, that we all have the power to transcend beyond the challenges we are going through.

With these new shifts and energetic waves, I am eager to integrate them into my work, into my cooking, my food, my creativity, my relationships and my family. I'm looking forward to the uncertainty ahead, as I continue shifting my life and my career into full alignment.

Reminding myself that these perspectives and stories wouldn't exist if it wasn't for this path. As big part of me that it is, a part that I've needed to claim is still only one glimpse into my painstakingly beautiful, and beautifully painstaking life.

NICOLE MENDES

Nicole Mendes is an International Traveling Chef. Originally from Massachusetts, she is a graduate of Johnson & Wales and the University of Massachusetts Amherst. With degrees in Culinary Arts, Sustainable Farming & Business, she has spent the past seven years working professionally in some of the most prestigious kitchens throughout Boston, from Rialto and to most Recently O Ya.

Once the pandemic happened, her life began to shift. She transitioned from restaurant life to working on a farm and managing farmers markets. Following her inner compass, her life took another turn when she was called to travel to Costa Rica to live on an off-grid permaculture farm and community in the middle of the jungle of Manzanillo. This then turned into cooking for retreats in the small town of Dominical on the opposite side of the country.

The culmination of these recent transitions and exposures to new ways of living and working has resulted in her quest for following and tuning into her intuition and questioning her higher purpose. She has been on a path of inner work, tapping into her spiritual guides in order to navigate life more gracefully, all with the intention to become more closely aligned to her most authentic self. Ultimately, this has allowed her to integrate more consciously into her role as a chef, farmer, and light being of the world. She describes her deep passion for food as one of the best ways to break down the barriers between people, opening them up to love, and nourishment all while offering a glimpse into her life.

Connect with Nicole at https://www.instagram.com/transcendentraveler.

CHAPTER 13

Dreams Don't Work Unless You Do

Sally Green

A Near Death Experience

When I was 18 months old, I reached out and grabbed a boiling pot of water off the stove. I was burned on my underarm, side and leg. While at the hospital, I developed a staph infection and went into a coma with a high fever. My grandmother hired a woman from the church who was a nurse to sit with me overnight when the family left. The nurse would lay hands on me and pray. After two days, the doctor called my parents in to update them on my condition. My Aunt Ginger went with them for support. The doctor told them the prognosis was not good. They didn't expect me to live through the night. The doctor asked a priest to come in the morning to give me last rites. My Aunt Ginger fainted.

The next morning, the nurse called my parents to tell them that my fever broke overnight. A week later I was heading home. Of course I don't remember any of this, but I have been told this story throughout my life. I share this story because I have always felt a connection to spirit. I have always been in awe of the power of prayer. Despite being given a dire prognosis, I survived thanks to the prayers of those around me. This experience has stayed with me throughout my life and has shown me the importance of faith in times of adversity.

Life Happens

In the years since, I have often thought about that experience and what might have happened if I had not survived. Why did I live? Was there something I was supposed to do with my life? How could I discover my true purpose? Though these questions have lingered with me for many years, I never really pursued the answers. Life has a way of happening and, before I knew it, years had gone by. Then in 2006 I had a spiritual awakening of sorts. A series of events led me to believe that it was finally time to start searching for the answers to those long-ago questions.

These past sixteen years I have been on a spiritual journey. It started when I helped create a bible study for teens and has taken me into the world of publishing and helping people share their stories. I have had the honor of working with some incredible people who have overcome some unbelievable challenges. Each story is unique and powerful in its own way. It is a reminder that no matter what we are going through, we are not alone. I am so grateful for this journey and all that it has taught me about myself, others, and most importantly how the holy spirit moves in our life.

As far back as I can recall, I have always had a sense that there is a higher power. This belief has been a source of comfort and strength for me throughout the years. Whenever I am faced with difficulties or feel lost, I have always turned to prayer. And while I have not always received the answers, I always felt better.

For a long time I prayed for answers and clarity about my purpose in life, but nothing seemed to come. I became frustrated and discouraged, wondering if there was something wrong with me. However, I eventually realized that I was trying to force my spiritual journey instead of letting it flow in its own way. Once I relaxed and allowed myself to be open to whatever might happen, I began to notice small signs and messages from the universe.

Trusting My Intuition

In 2006, I kept hearing a voice in my head telling me to ask my friend about the bible study she was taking. When I did, she not only told me about the bible study, but also shared that there were members of her group praying for a teen bible study. I became really excited because my daughter was a pre-teen and I told my friend I would love to have my daughter be part of a bible study like that.

I am so grateful that I followed my intuition and asked my friend about the bible study. If I hadn't, I would have missed out on an incredible opportunity for my daughter – and for myself. I ended up joining that prayer group, and became the missing piece they needed to create "B.O.B." Break Open the Bible, a bible study for middle school students.

Since that time, I have learned to trust that voice and trust my intuition. Intuition is our God-given guide that helps us make decisions in life. Through intuition, we can receive guidance, direction, and answers to our prayers. Intuition is a spiritual gift that we all have access to – we just need to learn how to connect with it and use it wisely.

Taking Action

In 2012, someone I had met through my bible study journey asked me to take a lay speaking class with her. I told her I was a bit apprehensive and that the thought of standing up in front of a group of people and giving a sermon frightened me. She told me to pray about it and that she would email me all the information. Something about the opportunity wouldn't let me sleep. That night, I tossed and turned and couldn't get the idea out of my head. I kept thinking about speaking and being able to share my faith with others. So I got up and did some research. My heart was telling me to take the class, but my head was looking for excuses because it was scary and out of my comfort zone.

I Googled what a lay speaker's responsibilities were and realized that this was something I could see myself doing. I opened her email and looked at the cost of the class. It was being subsidized by her church and was very affordable. Then I looked at the schedule and thought, "Surely I won't be able to fit it into my busy life." The classes were on Saturday mornings and I was totally free. The next morning I spoke with my husband about it. If he said "no," I would have my excuse. He thought it was a wonderful idea and told me I would be an amazing speaker.

So, despite my initial reluctance, I took the plunge and signed up for the class. It was one of the best decisions I ever made. Not only did I meet some amazing people, but I also had the opportunity to share my faith with others in a very powerful way. It also gave me the opportunity and encouragement to speak in front of people. Sometimes taking action is scary, but it is always worth it in the end.

Around the same time I began taking action and exploring my creative side, I started taking online acrylic paint classes. Getting lost while painting became a spiritual experience and I loved it. I suddenly had a passion and outlet that allowed me to be completely present and in the moment. I was no longer worrying about the future or dwelling on the past. I was creating something beautiful in the here and now. The sense of peace and joy that came from this creative process was something I had long forgotten. It was then that I realized that it is important to make time for activities that bring us joy. When we do, we open ourselves up to limitless possibilities.

I began teaching what I was learning in my art classes and inviting friends and family over for paint nights. It became a fun way to catch up with friends and we had a blast creating together. One of my friends recommended me to the activity director at her mom's retirement home, and I began teaching there. I desperately wanted to switch careers, and in November of 2019 I decided I wanted to make a career of teaching art classes. I began researching and connecting with other women who had successful paint & sip businesses. I created a business plan, contacted other retirement homes in my community, ordered business cards and started buying supplies. In January of 2020, I was all set to begin. I scheduled Saturday morning coffee and canvas classes in my church basement, and monthly Friday night Paint-n-sips. I sent emails to all of my friends and contacted a bunch of nonprofits about organizing a paint night fundraiser. I was excited to be following my passion. Then in March, you know what happened, the pandemic hit and all my paint classes were canceled.

I had a decision to make. I could sit in my disappointment or I could take action. At this point, I was a mess. I needed to make a change, so I did.

Transforming Worlds

Everything we go through in life – the good and the bad – is preparing us for what is yet to come. Change is inevitable, but it is also what helps us grow. As we learn how to transform our own lives, we can also transform the lives of others. We all have the power to make a difference in the world. It starts with making a commitment to ourselves and to our own personal growth. When we do that, everything else falls into place. We become more confident, more resilient, and more capable of handling whatever life throws our way.

I embarked on a journey of self-care and self discovery. I began eating healthier and taking daily walks with my husband and daughter. I shut off the television and read self-improvement books instead. I began my mornings with meditation and prayer. One evening I was offered the opportunity to write a chapter in a collaboration book on entrepreneurship. I jumped at the chance and began looking for ways to leverage the opportunity. I started reaching out to the other authors in the book and began connecting with them. I registered for their online courses, joined summits they were speaking at, and attended networking events they were hosting. I made sure to raise my hand and ask questions so they knew who I was.

I was so excited about being a part of the first book that I registered for another one. One of the authors I met was Lynda Sunshine West. She was hosting a networking event and I started attending them. Lynda ran a women's business mastermind that I joined. From there, she offered me the opportunity to be in two books she was publishing and I jumped at the chance. In less than a year, I had contributed to four #1 International bestselling collaboration books. I was over the moon.

After working with Lynda on the two books, she asked me to join her publishing company. I saw this as an opportunity of a lifetime. My heart has always been in service and writing is how I heal from things that happen in life and grow mentally and spiritually. The thought of being able to offer that service to others made my heart sing. I love being part of this company because every day brings new challenges - but nothing beats getting those emails saying "thank you" after we've helped someone write and share their story.

A Future So Bright I Gotta Wear Shades!

It is an honor to work for Action Takers Publishing. In many ways, it feels like we're on the cusp of something big - and I'm excited to be a part of it. Lynda and I are both passionate about helping writers share their stories, and we're always looking for new and innovative ways to improve the publishing process. I believe that staying focused and continuing to move in the direction of our dreams, there's a bright future ahead of us.

I am confident that I can learn a lot and contribute to the company's success. It's exciting to be able to work with a wide variety of people from all over the world. I believe that this experience will help me develop both professionally and personally. I am looking forward to the challenges and opportunities that lie ahead.

The bottom line is that you have everything you need to achieve any dream that you want. All it requires is learning how to trust your intuition, taking action, and being willing to change the world – starting with your own. It sounds simple, but it's not. It takes courage and faith to overcome self-doubt and stay committed.

Trying to stay focused on your goals can be tough when life keeps getting in the way. It's easy to get comfortable and just become a couch potato, but that's not what life is about. Life is about growth and change, so if you're not moving forward, then you're falling behind. If you want something bad enough, it's time to take that leap of faith and go after it. Dreams don't work unless you do.

SALLY GREEN

Sally Green is the Vice President of Author Development at Action Takers Publishing. She works with writers to help them develop their stories and become bestselling authors. Action Takers Publishing specializes in themed anthology or collaboration books where each person writes a chapter and becomes part of a community of like–minded authors. In addition to collaborative books, they also publish solo books.

Sally is an Inspirational Speaker, a multiple-times International Bestselling Author, and is in the process of writing her own book titled, *The Self-Care Rockstar* due to launch in 2023. She is the creator of the Self-Care Rockstar program, where she is hired to empower women to grow spiritually and become the rockstars of their own life.

In her spare time, Sally enjoys painting and teaches acrylic paint classes to local senior centers, women's groups, and children's summer camps.

Connect with Sally at www.ActionTakersPublishing.com.

CHAPTER 14

POWER of Growth, Aligned-Growth, and Growth Mindset in Everyday Life

Sharon Rose Wallen

"In everything give thanks, for this is the will of God in Christ Jesus concerning you." 1 Thessalonians 5:18 KJV

"To: Ms. Wallen

From: TTC-Fridge

Thank you!

For teaching me.

For making me a fridge.

For trying to give these kids manners.

For being humble during any situation.

For believing in our dreams and goals and motivations (except robbery).

For coming to work every day putting up with our foolishness (meaning having to waste your time, lol).

For lifting us up to our goals.

For making us feel important." "Flip page for motivational line."

"You may have been called "nothing" when you've had nothing. You may have been picked on when you shared your liking of something you wanted to grind for. But those people are those who missed their goals. You might change the color of your hair. You might change your shoes. But you are still you and you are going to work hard to climb that mountain to your goal and be successful. Some might say, "that's impossible!" Why not set a world record from it? You are powerful. Never let someone tell you that you are weak. Never let someone say that you are too out of shape. People will misjudge you. Ignore them. You be you. You do you and you will succeed." Past Student Torin, 10 years old

"My positive attitude starts flowing when I enter this classroom." 12/16/13 Past Student Adrian, 10 years old

"SUCCESS because of Ms. Wallen

Ms. Wallen, you show us how to be successful. Teaching us reading, writing, and science and letting us tweak our work and showing us Gifted Goals and Objectives. You show us our goals in education. You teach us ways of life and how to write, showing us to have success not to be a mess." Past Student Valerie Harper, 10 years old

"Mrs. Wallen,

Thank you for thinking of my precious Olivia. It is truly a pleasure to work with such a wonderful partner, mentor, and friend." Love, Jennifer Meneses, (My Co-Teacher)

Self-Worth – Taking Action in the Face of Adversity

"Everyone needs a house to live in, a supportive family is what builds a home." www.the pioneerwoman.com. My maternal grandmother listened to her favorite Soap Opera story, Dulcimina, on a transistor radio (portable and handheld) when she visited our home. She individualized treats for us; for example, my dad loved naseberry fruits so she brought them specifically, "these are for Mr. Wallen." She verbalized her care for each person in our family and in his or her unique way. We knew Granny loved us. Her husband, Grandpa Joe (Papi), was less verbal, but he bought us Jamaican Patties with Coco-bread and soft drinks (Desnoes and Geddes soda, D&G beverages) and fresh snapper, which my grandmother escovitched with white rice for us. My favorite seafood is Lobster because Granny cooked us Curried Lobster with Rice as everyday dishes when we visited her in her home in Black River, St. Elizabeth. My paternal grandparents were similarly active in our lives. Dad's mother baked us our own birthday cakes to our preferences. I liked mine with fruits. I had sisters who preferred their cake plain. Granddad Herbert Wallen gave us our most memorable family pet, a puppy. He also had a joke expression he said to us when our summer vacation ended, "Your free-paper burn," which meant summer holidays were over. All those experiences were before 17 years old, my age when my family migrated to the United States of America. As an immigrant teenager from Jamaica, West Indies, my family, consisting of my parents with five daughters, arrived in America with strong familial foundations, traditions, support, and willingness to face our new challenges and enjoy opportunities before us.

The decades of my life have been a journey of faith and trust in my Higher Power, goal-setting, striving to achieve those goals, lots of laughter along the way, and problem-solving strategies to understand social-emotional challenges or work through tough interpersonal relationships. For example, early in my teaching career, my mentor had a ton of ideas and resources for Open House/Back-to-School Night for parents, yet she copied one of my ideas as part of her presentation and that really startled me: an experienced teacher already had so many ideas yet found it necessary to take a Newbie's signature idea. Another great colleague and mentor had what is called a difficult personality.

She was so kind and funny at times, but very caustic other times. She was in control of the day's social-emotional climate for everyone she encountered. I remember constantly trying to figure out, Sharon, what are you experiencing? *Codependent No More* by Melody Beattie and *Toxic Work: How to Overcome Stress, Overload, and Burnout and Revitalize Your Career* by Barbara Bailey Reinhold were among my guidebooks that shed light on what I was experiencing and added substance with clarity as fodder for my early work life and personal growth.

I was born in Kingston, Jamaica, to a Registered Nurse and a Police Officer who attained Assistant Commissioner of Police status by the end of his 46 years career. My parents raised their five daughters in a faith-based, Christ-centered, God-fearing home. The ages of my siblings and I span over Baby Boomers and Gen X generations.

Trusting Intuition about my next has been following a guiding light. New to America, as a teenager with my High School Diploma, I still needed to be vetted with GED for American documentation required for my college applications. All those necessities were expedited within ten months when I began my Bachelor's Degree in Spring of 1978. One hundred and twenty-two credits seemed a long distance away, yet I graduated within the 4-year limit with 132 credits.

The hand of God directing me has transformed how I make decisions, energized my faith, and gives me peace on my daily journey today. The mercies of God are always present.

Self-Efficacy – Took Control of My Life and Made a Change

Only 3% of America's teachers are National Board Certified. Today, National Board Certified teachers are still rare in classrooms across America. National Board for Professional Teaching Standards is America's proven tool for identifying quality teaching. However, it is not required but rather, this advanced certification process is voluntary. Its merits include that it's a measure to accurately identify teacher quality and research consistently documents that NBCTs advance and increase student learning to the tune of at least two months learning gains. Those are consistent findings for decades when queries are pursued regarding the efficacy of NBPTS.

I attained this elite certification status in 2001 and have maintained it through two renewal timeframes, even most recently in 2021 during my retirement. The majority of my 32-year career in teaching I've been a National Board Certified Teacher. Earlier in this writing I mentioned mentors. Well, it was one of those colleagues who approached me about pursuing that certification and encouraged me to attempt the grueling process. The support that a colleague believed I had the ability and believed in me and that I was worthy of that honor wasn't lost on me.

What's the pinnacle standard in your line of work, career, choice of pursuit? Seek it out. Try to attain it. Not because you're in comparison with anyone, but because bliss, well-being, optimum satisfaction, and self-actualization are like four legs of a table on which you can rest your life's gratification, proverbial and realistic awards, and your gains. Never give up. Pursue your dreams. Steve Jobs once said, "Your work is going to fill a large part of your life, and the only way to be truly satisfied is to do what you believe is great work." Not only do I agree with Jobs' statement here, but my career experiences showed the benefits of my holistic approach to teaching. I had the style that students and their families were my clients and I needed to bring them the best customer service for that school year and, for that day. Early in my career also, a veteran teacher advised me, "Always remember that every year is a new set of seven-year-olds (talking about second grade) that's coming to your class. Keep yourself and your skills sharp and alert to give your best to that new group of children." Looking back over my career, that was great advice that I was given in the early years of my work.

From the quotes that opened this chapter, my life story, you'll notice it's my past students who expressed during the school year and at the end of their school year with me, just how classroom culture, teaching and learning work experiences, interpersonal relationships, and reflective feedback impacted their own lives. Their written reflections highlighted and teach many attributes of human interaction: 1) they are children, but their minds, brains, emotions, feelings, reasonings, are active in the classroom; 2) they know when they are respected and challenged to their higher capacity and higher ability; and 3) young children can identify, verbalize the dimensions of themselves that were supported, opened, enhanced, allowed to bloom, allowed to shine, allowed to flourish, be seen, expressed, and they were able to express gratitude to me repeatedly, over and over, of my influence and the impact of my presence, outlook, care, and work on their life throughout that school year. I think my biggest take-away from my job, life's work, career, is the feedback I've received from the young lives I've worked with.

Some honors and awards I've received throughout my career include: 2003-2004 Who's Who Among America's Teachers: Honoring Our Nation's Most Respected Teachers (National Dean's List Student); 2005-2006 Outstanding American Teachers: Recognizing Educators Who Have Made a Positive Difference in Their Students' Lives (National Honor Roll Student); 2018-2019 Who's Who in America as an individual who possesses professional integrity, demonstrates outstanding achievement in my respective field, and has made innumerable contributions to society as a whole. In December 2021, I received the Albert Nelson Marquis Lifetime Achievement Award for achieving career longevity and for demonstrating unwavering excellence in my chosen field of work, education. Those are pinnacles of achievement recognition. They all started because various of my past students who attained National Dean's List status and National Honor Roll status were interviewed by these leaders and the students identified me among the teachers who inspired, motivated, and impacted their aspirations, achievements, lives, and future. Fact is, I taught these children in Elementary School and they left me by ten and eleven years old. They had many teachers in middle school and high school who were more current to their ages when they achieved their honors. These results prove Psychologist Erik Erikson's 8 Stages of Psychosocial Development work that school age needs of Industry vs Inferiority are critically important and should be nurtured in America's classrooms and other social settings such as families and neighborhoods. Erikson's stages of Infancy (Trust vs. Mistrust) and Early Childhood (Autonomy vs. Shame and Doubt) precede school age. I believe an effective classroom culture of nurturance, Emotional Intelligence strategies, Positive Peace strategies woven with essentials of Dignity can make up for teaching and learning deficiencies in the past. I also believe that it's each teacher's professional responsibility to provide a caring, empathetic, and respectful learning environment for their learners. Psychologist Abraham Maslow's work on Motivation and Personality emphasizes the importance of meeting basic needs before anyone, including children, can pay attention or be motivated to meet their other needs of the hierarchy.

Self-Regulation – Gut Feelings and Learning to Trust My Intuition

Participating in this Wickedly Smart Women project was an example of my trusting my gut feelings that God, my Higher Power, gave me an open door towards my goals of National Publicity for my message and my recent book, *Grateful Reflections Journal*. Throughout my life, I've found that intuition has been a silent pilot. My intentions, desires, preferences, dreams, and goals have been realized to mastery, realization, high-quality resolution, which all symbolized for me an eagle's eye. Though unseen, intuition for me has been a focused dominant factor that pulled me to victory, triumph, expansion, and more. Intuition, my inner watchful eye, has been reliable because I check the circumstance

I'm facing, decision to be made, problem to be solved, against my biblical beliefs and values, psychological standards, my moral compass, past experiences, wants and desires, my comfort zone, then I choose. I do not like physical, moral, nor emotional pain, so I usually carefully weigh risks involved for the decision: if I decide the cost is worth it or if I'm willing to learn the lesson I'll gain from the new experience, then I go forward with the adventure.

Similarly, an eagle's symbolism is relevant here for the strategy that I've used throughout my lifetime. Recognizing the quiet voice of my strengths, beliefs, values, goals, dreams, and weighing that against the odds of the opportunities before me, for the most part, has given me strong faith and a rewarding life with deep satisfaction to face my future. Aligned-Growth has provided me a peaceful journey throughout my walk on Earth. Periods of tough relationships and hard knocks against my optimistic, positive, growth mindset propelled me to seek additional information, research and learn, depart and pull away, stay my course, tweak an action or an idea, be patient, stop negative associations, modify an attitude, humble myself and carry on.

I remember late in my career when I was asked to abandon my classroom to move in with another teacher to maintain my grade level assignment or choose to work in a lower grade level. I remember telling my principal, "Change is constant, change is inevitable, so I'll move into the other teacher's classroom and co-teach the class with her." That was not easy to live through and that school year I even experienced bouts of High Blood Pressure when that's never in my health records. However, experiences such as those show what trying to stabilize your identity and norm in a high-pressured, pressure-cooker experience can destabilize health or other conditions. I remember clearly when I began to use the phrase, "that's not like you, Sharon…" and I also began to dress casually. Those new action steps allowed me to end the school year mentally strong and in good health. Aligned-Growth, my daily behaviors aligned to my beliefs and values, led to resilience, overcoming odds, progress towards self-actualization, my experiencing peak performance, and an overall achievement of self-mastery.

Life is not easy. However, in the few decades of my life's journey, Growth is constant. I've also found that openness to a Growth Mindset, talent, abilities, and beliefs can be positively enhanced, grow and change and lead to purposeful living. I've also found that the technique of Aligned-Growth, where one's self-awareness, actions, and outlook, fuel one's motives and aspirations, and leads to a life of satisfaction and happiness achieved by beating the odds and overcoming challenges to attain dreams and goals.

SHARON ROSE WALLEN

Sharon Rose Wallen is a Lifetime Achievement Award Recipient 2021 and a member of America's elite 3% of teachers, a National Board Certified Teacher. She worked for 32 years in Elementary Education for America's 4th largest school district. Her work has influenced children to achieve leadership in extra-curricular service learning experiences, believe in themselves as successful learners, and create lasting ambitions to maximize their potential and positively impact their life and future. She has degrees in Psychology, Sociology, Elementary Education, and Early Childhood Generalist. Sharon has answers that build resilience and foster emotional and physical health despite today's troubled times. Sharon is the Author of Grateful Reflections Journal, an open-ended stems to foster independence, personal growth, and mental wellness.

Connect with Sharon here: https://gratefulreflectionsjournal.com

CHAPTER 15

From Outside Sales to Multi-Million-Dollar Company Owner

by Stacey Magovern

My name is Stacey Magovern, a born and raised Texas girl. As the daughter of Lin Rushing, I like to say I was born an entrepreneur. My mother opened her first retail store when I was just 5 months old. While she worked hard meeting and dressing the Big Country's women, I grew up in the back room eventually wrapping gifts for customers and cleaning out dressing rooms. In my family, getting a college degree was not an option; it was a mandate. After graduating from Cooper High School, I left Abilene for a few years to achieve my Bachelor of Arts in Communications from National University in California. After a short time, I realized California was no place for this Texas girl and returned to Abilene. Immediately, I went to work for my mother, who had grown her business to five retail stores. I worked the floor selling everything from skiwear and cosmetics to Boy Scout® uniforms and eveningwear. I also accompanied my mother on every trip to the Dallas Apparel Mart. My Mother was tough. She had high expectations and every employee had to justify their salary with meeting or exceeding her sales goals.

I always knew I wanted to own my own business one day. The funny part is I never considered leaving Abilene. When a lingerie store went up for sale just down the street from my mother's shopping center, I had to have it. At the time a lot of people in my small town thought my mother bought it for me, but nothing could be further from the truth. In fact, she even refused to co-sign on a loan. Luckily, I hadn't screwed up my credit in college like many of my friends, so I was able to get an SBA loan for a portion of the purchase price and then I negotiated a final payment for the business six months after purchase. This was my first real experience in business negotiations and really thinking outside the box to make something happen. This was impressive for a 23-year-old and I often think back on this in my business today. I learned a lot in my lingerie business, especially from failure. Yes, that business totally failed. There were many reasons for the failure, and the biggest reason was that at the same time a national chain lingerie store began opening in every shopping mall across America, Abilene included. They could sell lingerie for the same price I could buy it.

After closing my retail store, I spent the next 15 years in outside sales in the corporate world. The realization that I could go get sales and not sit back in a store and wait for people to come to me was life changing. I was extremely successful in outside sales consistently winning awards, trips and eventually managing my own sales team. However, that yearning to own my own business never went away. Growing someone else's dream was never my end goal. I knew eventually I would find my next big adventure. I just didn't know when or where.

In 2005, I met and married the love of my life, Michael Magovern, a police officer. We moved to the Dallas-Fort Worth metroplex. He continued to work as a police officer and I got another outside sales position. During this time as a police wife, I learned a lot about police officers. These amazing people who put their lives on the line every day in most departments are paid very little. They rely on off-duty work to make ends meet. I watched my husband try to supplement our income with off-duty work here and there with no real guarantee of work and very random opportunities.

That's when my next big idea came to me. I wanted to start a management company for police and off-duty work. How great would it be if each officer could schedule their off-duty work and know exactly how much additional income they would have each month? It made perfect sense to me. My husband had the police contacts and with my sales experience I could get the clients. I spent the next two years working on my idea while maintaining a full-time job, raising two boys, and running a household. I sacrificed every minute of free time working on this business idea.

I started by forming my LLC, Point Blank Safety Services. I began reaching out to highway construction companies because I knew they use off-duty police for their projects. This became my "WHY." I knew there had to be a better way to connect police with work and clients with police officers. Those two years were hard and many times I thought about giving up, but I am thankful now for the time I spent trying to create a business because I now respect my business and how hard I worked to get here. I truly believe if I would have had this success in my 20s, I wouldn't appreciate it as much as I do. Life is all about timing.

There are a lot of lessons I've learned along the way. Trusting my intuition is one of them. In addition to that, I'd like to share with you some of the things I've discovered along this journey to help me reach the success I have today.

Find a problem in your industry and solve it

My number one strategy for a business is that you must find a problem in your industry and solve it. My business does this. I learned quickly that construction companies were typically using a full-time person just to hire, schedule, and pay officers for their projects. My company could come in and take that over. One point of contact and one invoice for everything. This allowed the construction companies to free up that full-time position for something revenue generating. I could see the light bulbs going off in my head as I presented my services to potential clients. This is key to creating a business that is scalable. This is when my life changed.

In September of 2014, I was in the bathroom getting ready for work just like any other day when the doorbell rang. It was FedEx® with a package for Point Blank Safety Services. At that point my business hadn't received any packages. Believe it or not, I opened up the package and just about fainted. There was a $1.5 million contract sitting inside that box. It was to use our pool of police officers for traffic control on a new highway construction project in Dallas, Texas. I did it! I created a real company, one that would help hundreds of police officers and their families. To say the next few weeks were a blur is an understatement. As they say, be careful what you wish for. You just might get it. I was so focused on my WHY, that I just kept going. I knew I had something, but had no idea when it would break loose. THAT was the big break we needed.

There is power in thinking big

My second strategy for business is to think big. You will never scale a business on small clients and one-time deals. Yes, all sales do add up, but you must bag the elephants to keep your business growing and moving forward. I know this can be intimidating, especially when you're just getting started and you're no more than an idea and a business card. However, if you believe in yourself and your vision, others will too. Don't be scared to put yourself out there and talk to the big players in your field. Everyone starts somewhere. I think people admired my tenacity and the big vision for my company and that is what got me the meetings I needed to win the large contract. In sales, I always ask myself what is the worst thing that could happen if I contact this potential client. The answer is simple, they say "no." When you think of it in those terms, it's not so scary. Besides, "NO" never really means "NO," it just means they don't have enough information yet. I have never had a meeting with a potential client that I didn't learn something from even if I didn't close the deal.

Outsourcing is key

Okay. Now let's talk about what to do next. You won the deal and you're now a real company. One of the most important strategies is to outsource. You are only one person. You cannot do it all. The key to outsourcing is knowing what you are good at. I am good at sales and business development and I love it. I'm not good at bookkeeping or scheduling. My husband does all the scheduling for my company and I outsource many other things. I hear a lot of business owners say they can't afford to outsource. You will never have a scalable business if you don't outsource. Outsourcing goes hand in hand with another strategy which is to surround yourself with other successful people. If you do this, you will find the right resources in which to outsource. The first place to start finding successful people to connect with is in networking groups. Most Chambers of Commerce have networking groups you can attend. A networking group is merely a group of professionals that come together to help grow each other's businesses.

Be the expert

Another strategy that is a must is to be an expert at what you do. Create the perfect process for your service. In my business, I knew that the pain for the clients was having to deal directly with dozens of police officers. I also knew the pain for the officers was not having a set schedule of when they work and not having steady off-duty jobs. My husband and I created a process that solves all of this. He handles scheduling so he sends out an availability calendar at the beginning of each month. The officers mark the days they are available for work. He matches the officers' availability with the client requests for staffing. This allows him to create a work schedule up to two weeks in advance. With this process, we can tell clients how many officers we have available and officers are able to know exactly when they work and plan life and family around that. It also helps on the sales side, so I know when we need more contracts and when we need to recruit more officers. I have been told many times what sets us apart from other companies is our unique scheduling system. It is also the reason we have officers that have been with us since day one.

Create a company culture

From our first day working our first contract, I knew for this to work I must create a culture in that made people want to work with me and for me. My husband, a police officer for over 15 years, said to me that our motto should be "Family first." To be honest, I didn't really agree with that at first, but when I saw the officers' reactions when they had to call off from a shift and they were told, "It's okay. Your family always comes first," I could feel the relief in their voices. Nobody wants to work where there is constant fear of being written up, threatened or replaced. If you are working with professionals, they should be treated like professionals. When employees feel appreciated, they will work harder and stay longer. I also started in my second year of business holding an officer appreciation event every year. You can do the same type of things for employees and business partners. I always invite vendors and special clients to these events as well. Clients also want to feel appreciated.

Protect what you built

This strategy is one that many business owners forget. Protect what you built. I see so many people build a good business and then get complacent or arrogant thinking the success will never end. To protect what you have worked so hard to create is essential. You must always be adding clients to your sales funnel. Know your sales cycle. How long does it take you to acquire a new client and what steps does it take and at what cost? Never assume a client won't leave; always be prepared if they do. At any given moment, you should know exactly where your next ten deals are coming from. You should also be constantly looking at ways to decrease expenses. I pull up my profit and loss statement every week and go over it. This helps me identify the best months, the largest expenses, and what the business is on track to make for the year. This tells me if I need to ramp up sales and how quickly. In the beginning, all new business owners are continually seeking knowledge. Don't let that stop. Keep learning every day. No matter how successful you are, you can still learn something new. A successful business is continually changing and adapting to business trends and the economy.

Be willing to work with the competition

The next strategy is one most people don't even consider. Be willing to work with your competitors. I know what you are thinking… Why? Because doing what is best for the client will get you more business. I can't tell you how many deals I have won because I offered to be the backup vendor. When a client says to me, "I already have a contract with your competitor." So many salespeople hear that and give up. Not me. I say, "That's great." Please just keep me in mind if they ever can't fill an order or you have issues. We have no problem being the backup for your project." When the client calls and we must service the account and they see our amazing process firsthand, we almost always end up winning the account. Remember, as I said earlier, "no" never means "no," it just means they don't have all the information. If you are not confident enough in your product or service to stand side by side with a competitor, you need to go back to strategy 5 and perfect your process.

Change your mindset

My final strategy for a successful business is that you must change your mindset. Once you become a business owner, you can no longer look at things like an employee. Success isn't a destination; it is a continuous journey. For example, an employee says, "That's not my job," where a business owner knows every job is their job. An employee gets a salary even on bad days. A business owner knows that if it doesn't succeed, people are out of work. An employee is ready to quit at 5pm and a business owner stays to make just one more call or send one more quote. This also refers to my second strategy, a business owner thinks BIG and has a vision, where a typical employee just wants to get paid for what they do. Once you stop thinking like an employee who just wants to make enough money to pay the bills, your business can really grow. When I started Point Blank Safety Services, I of course wanted to make enough money to support my family, but I saw past that to the hundreds of police officers I could also help support their families. Now I continue to work to keep contracts coming in because police officers need our services and clients love our services.

I hope this is what exactly you need to take that next step in your life and business. I want to help you release the fear of failure and go big and loud; make it happen. You are the only person that can change your life.

STACEY MAGOVERN

Stacey Magovern went from outside salesperson to running a multi-million-dollar company overnight. The wife of a police officer, Stacey's passion for helping families of law enforcement became her business.

She launched her company, Point Blank Safety Services, in 2012 with no way of knowing today her company would be one of the most successful traffic safety and security companies in Texas.

She used her success to pay it forward by founding a nonprofit, Blue Family Fund, that provides scholarships for First Responder dependents and financial aid to families of injured or fallen law enforcement officers. Stacey is not just the CEO and founder of these businesses, she is also a bestselling author, entrepreneur, and motivational speaker.

Stacey has been very blessed in her business and because of that she and her husband started a nonprofit called Blue Family Fund, Inc. They provide scholarships and financial assistance to families of First Responders. Please check them out and donate if you can at bluefamilyfund.org.

Learn more about Point Blank Safety at www.pointblanksafety.com.

CHAPTER 16

Across the Other Side of Intuition

Valeriia Hearn

When I was a little girl, I was certain that my life's purpose was to run away and join the circus to be a tightrope walker. That plan didn't work out. I've come back to that image of me as a tightrope walker once more. Don't worry, I promise you that I'm not planning to run away and join the circus...

It's just that Lyme disease has left me feeling like a tightrope walker who is just beginning to learn how to master the art of balance. There I am, flailing my arms left and right in a desperate attempt not to go down- which only causes me to lose my footing!

Sometimes you need to be quiet to listen to the child that is still inside of you. I know that a little girl in me - the tightrope walker - would have quite a few things to say to the grown-up version of the tightrope walker. Don't look down or you'll fall! Don't even *think* about falling... just think about what you DO WANT to do and DO IT! I know you will get across to the other side!

So, for the little girl in me who always wanted to join the circus, I'm going to stop thinking about falling and start focusing on getting across to the other side of the tightrope. If I do fall down, I've got an amazing safety net waiting with open arms to catch me – Creator of All That Is.

From my notes during my period of recovery.

- What is intuition?

- To be fully in – to – IT. Be fully connected to the very center of our Creation, to that spark inside our hearts.

- To be fully into LIFE in all of its forms and to always choose and accept yourself as the main character of this existence.

We are all born as intuitive people. As we all are unique, so is our intuition. For some of us, it's a "gut feeling" when we can physically feel a response from our body, sometimes it can be just knowing, or even visual images that we can experience consciously or in our dreams. When we pay attention, we can notice how Creator communicates with us through our hearts, and then we spend eternity learning how to always choose this voice over many others.

A major challenge that we all experience as a society today is our addiction to reason with everything; to have a conscious explanation for each decision we make. We choose to trust the outer world way more often than our inner world. Then we experience moments of frustration, depression and feel completely disconnected and lost, because in a core of it, we betray ourselves and God's light inside us.

Ironically, it's impossible to reason with intuitive guidance simply because you haven't walked this path yet. It's a process of learning and trusting fully until you reach your destination and receive validation. Some of us will spend our whole life mastering that skill, but it's in our power to make this process enjoyable despite all the obstacles we might face.

Early on I had to learn that being intuitive and trusting your intuition doesn't guarantee an easy life, free of challenge. In fact, it turned out to be completely opposite, especially when your inner voice sounds very different than the voice of society.

How often do we allow ourselves to connect to our hearts and truly feel and hear divine guidance? We rely on other people's opinions: parents, teachers, experts, doctors, etc. Don't get me wrong! It's wonderful to have all the knowledge and support we can receive in life, but what if your heart is telling you something completely opposite to what the majority thinks? Will you be able to remain strong and follow this little voice inside without even knowing where it's taking you?

A couple of years ago, I had to answer all these questions myself as I was learning how to trust my intuition in my biggest desire: to be alive and to have a quality, healthy life. While everyone around me thought that it was impossible for me.

Almost 10 years ago I first landed in Dulles International airport to begin my new life in America. It was an extremely hot August day. I remember being surprised by the dense, moist air that quickly filled my lungs when I first stepped outside the airport. I was filled with a sense of wonder inside my heart, just as the energy of the city was filled with a sense of rush and bustle. Believe it or not, even the road signs amazed me that day. Every single inch of the new land felt like home to me. What a joy it is to live and to be alive! I knew that my life was about to take a completely new turn. I was ready. I didn't know what I was really getting ready for at that time.

When we are young, we often do not think about the real value of our health. Even about the value of this wonderful moment we all call life. A couple of months after my relocation, I found myself unable to perform my usual activities. Every movement caused me a lot of pain. I began to have different allergic reactions here and there and developed strong food intolerance. My energy level was so low that I had to have a break each time after I took a shower. Indeed, my body was alerting me that something was wrong, but I had no idea how I could support it.

This was the beginning of my journey of learning what it means to truly trust my inner voice even despite all the social standards and "facts"; doctor after doctor I was hearing exact same thing "you are fine!," "everything looks normal, just make sure to drink more water," "you are young and healthy, you just seek attention," "stop making this up," "you should see physiatrist, there is nothing we can do for you here."

I felt devastated, scared, and betrayed by my own body, doctors, and even some family members. I started to question myself – perhaps it's really all in my head? Every time my inner voice would whisper back to me – "no, keep trying, don't give up! You will find the answer." I knew I had only two choices – to give up and trust others or stay connected and allow for my inner voice to guide me to the right place.

Believe me, it was not an easy decision to make. Especially when you deal with the medical community. I had to learn how to become my own advocate, how to do my own research and which questions to ask so my voice would be heard by others. It was one of the darkest and loneliest times in my life. The only thing that helped me to remain focused and consistent was my inner voice.

Later, I understood that it was the voice of the Creator coming through me. He believed in me even when I was losing my hope, always lifting me up and reminding me that our life is a wonder itself; and that I can have joy and happiness inside even through the pain and scared self. I was learning that suffering is optional, and that love, and light is permanent. I remember giving myself a promise: for as long as I am given just one more day to live, I will choose myself and I will remain connected to that little voice inside me. I know something is going on and I will find the answer.

Days and months went by and finally after a year of numerous ER visits, hundreds of doctor appointments, surgeries, and blood work,

I was fortunate enough to meet a doctor who guided me to the right tests and information. It felt like my struggle was over; I'm about to receive a proper diagnosis and I will be healed! I remember looking at my positive blood results, celebrating it because finally I had proof that my inner voice was right. It was not "all in my head."

"You have Chronic Lyme disease, multiple co-infections and heavy metals and mold intoxication." All of that sounded so foreign to me, and I didn't understand much during my first appointment. "Your journey will be long – there is no proven treatment for your condition at this moment and it's impossible to get rid of the infection complete-ly. We can only help you manage some of your symptoms and get your inflammation under control."

It was such a mixture of feelings inside me. On one hand, I was so happy to hear my diagnosis and to finally know what's going on with my body, and on the other hand, it sounded like no one understood how to help me to get better. I felt like a climber; while you are climbing up the mountain you are so focused and intentional, you ignore pain and discomfort and do not allow yourself to feel tired or pity yourself. Then when you reach the peak you suddenly realize how heavy your legs are, that you are exhausted and hungry. Even more – it's a rainy day so you cannot even enjoy the view for which you were hoping.

I knew there is no guarantee in life – we never know for how long we've come here and if we are going to enjoy all the phases of our life in this mortal body. After receiving my diagnosis, I wanted to research as much as I could about the condition and all the treatment options. At that time, it was not much information and research available for patients who had the infection long-term. I was heartbroken to find out that a lot of patients die from this condition, simply because the treatment itself is so rough on the system or they didn't receive help on time and the infection had spread too much.

I remember lying in bed, having my conversation with God. That night I kept asking him: is it my time to go? Honestly, I felt like a burden. For society, I "didn't look sick enough," I was often judged as anti-social and even "lazy" person; if you are currently dealing with Lyme disease, you know what I am talking about. It was impossible for me to plan anything because I simply had no idea if my body would be strong enough that day to perform even minimal activity. My "norm" was too far away from the life I was dreaming about.

I was lost and disconnected from my heart. Fear overcame me and all I wanted was to finally be pain-free. It felt too long. For so many years I had pain every single day, without any breaks. My body became my own prison. Perhaps, my intuition is wrong this time and I am not being able to recover fully. I no longer believed that it was possible for me to get better; I had a lot of medical debts, all the treatment I received so far only made me feel worse and I knew I was not moving towards my healing. In fact, I felt like I was quickly going down the hill. I felt like I've lost myself.

Again, that little voice came through my heart to remind me that all the other voices: of my fears, doctors and even the voice of my illness is not the highest truth, it's NOT who I am. I got a beautiful reminder that I should surrender to love fully, allow my body to receive the healing light of unconditional love and keep searching, because there is a better option available for me. "Don't allow others to dictate to you what your body can and cannot do. Your purpose here is to master connection with Creator to understand His true power." Yes, healing IS possible, and for me too.

I am not my illness, and I should focus on my journey, not the destination. I don't know when and how I will restore my wholeness but for as long as I trust and move forward, I am on the right path. I was reminded of how loved I am, that my angels and Creator support and surround me fully. Even when my legs cannot move, I have the luxury of SEEING and being able to celebrate sunshine by looking at it through the window in my bedroom. Gratitude is a choice, and I chose to connect to that frequency instead. I knew I must learn how to love myself fully even through that disease, even though all the pain and obscurity of my condition.

I decided to learn more about holistic approach to wholeness, I realized that it's important to restore it, rather than to treat my symptoms. I got into meditation, I learned how to work with the subconscious mind, and committed to listen to my intuition and connect to my heart daily, visualizing the light and love of the Creator restoring my physical body. It was so powerful, that even my pain would dissolve in it fully for the duration of my meditative practice. I learned how to LIVE fully as I am already healthy.

Shortly after I found a holistic clinic that specializes solely in Lyme disease. With the help of my family, friends and even strangers we raised much needed funds for me to be able to receive healing and learn about Dr. Klinghardt's philosophy. For the first time since I got sick, I was able to have support and validation from doctors. I learned that it's very important to work on all five levels of our existence to heal fully: physical, energy, mental, intuitive, and spiritual. That the most important work is done between you and Creator. Because there is always a limit to what we, as human beings, can do. So, I continued to master my connection with Creator.

The first results were almost instantaneous; when I got home, I didn't have any physical pain for a few days for the first time in many years! I knew I was guided there because I was ready; I gained all the wisdom and collected every lesson that disease had taught me. Of course, It took me a few more years to reach complete recovery: I had to change my mindset, lifestyle, work a lot on my limiting beliefs, as well as continue to support my physical body with supplements, proper nutrition, and body work. My body and soul were restoring every day.

I learned a lot about different healing modalities; first, as a client and later as a practitioner and instructor. My inner voice guided me to the right people, books, and classes. By that time, I learned how to trust fully without second guessing it. I was slowly returning to my true self. I learned the true power of Unconditional Love, and that when we are fully connected to the Creator everything is possible. I was able to witness my own miraculous healing. Today, I have the privilege to connect my clients to the infinite possibilities in the process of their personal healing and transformation as a Connect mE coach at YU2SHINE™ and I am so grateful for that.

VALERIIA HEARN

"A sacred illness is one that educates us and alters us from the inside out, provides experiences and therefore knowledge that we could not possibly achieve in any other way, and aligns us with a life path that is, ultimately, of benefit to ourselves and those around us." ~ Deena Metzger

Valeriia Hearn is a Connect mE coach, Quantum Touch practitioner, Thetahealing© instructor and Free-mE™ EFT instructor. She hopes her story will encourage those who might doubt their inner guidance to continue moving forward with faith. She knows that the resistance of the world may be too great for you to remain strong and confident. You must remember that Creator is much bigger, higher, and stronger than you and even stronger than all the voices around you. He will certainly give you enough strength to endure when you are ready to accept His help and turn inward to discover yourself and connect to YOUR inner truth.

She brings to your awareness that you are never alone on this journey, even though sometimes it might feel and look that way. The choice is always yours: whether to accept the support and help of the higher power, or remain a victim of circumstances, endlessly betraying your-self for the sake of the majority. Valeriia's intention for this chapter is to show you how amazing your life will be and already is when you choose to connect to your intuition. Overcome internal and external limitations, shed excessive husks, and discover the renewed light of your soul, which can illuminate the path for many people around you.

May you discover the courage to connect to LOVE always.

Connect with Valeriia at

https://yu2shine.com/valeriia-nechyporenko-connect-me-coach/

CHAPTER 17

Just at the Right Time...

Victoria Rader

"You have to call Randy," – the feeling was subtle yet persistent. Randy is my husband who was teaching in China at the time. When he picked up, it became quickly apparent that due to a severe jetlag he slept through his alarm and, had I not called, he would have missed his class. There it goes. Just a small miracle.

This small coincidence of someone's name popping into our mind is something all of us can relate to and happens to be one of the greatest tools of our creative mind, our intuition. In my seminars I talk about six mental faculties as a collective mind-set: intuition, imagination, perception, reason, memory, and will. All six either work together to expand our purpose on this planet or collide in chaos to keep us confused. They either compete against each other or work in harmony, creating a life full of miracles.

There are one too many painful times when I chose to ignore my intuition and used my reason to convince myself otherwise. I could write volumes titled *The Times I Ignored my Intuition*. There were many small incidents like ignoring a simple quiet feeling *to not put this dish under the water* reasoning that it has been out of the oven long enough to have cooled off, to only have the glass pan completely shatter and pulling the glass shreds out of my hand, my hair and then crawling and collecting them from the tiniest crevices of our wood floor.

There were greater ones when I ignored a subtle feeling to first *not* go into a business partnership and then to *let it go* and instead reasoned and justified that the friendship was the most important thing and to preserve the friendship, I had to make the business partnership work. When the news came announcing that this same partner was no longer interested in staying in business with me, I was staring at my email in complete disbelief. After the years of close friendship, there were cutting words of the cold detached business-like jargon leaving me feeling gutted emotionally and strained due to broken obligations financially. I called. I cried. I panicked. I paid back the money owed to clients based on non-performance of obligations made.

Only, wait for it, to repeat it again… and again… Losing first just $4,000… then $70,000… then $35,000… in different business ventures, but following the same path. I would choose to ignore the same subtle intuitive feeling that made no logical sense, overriding it with logic, data, and reason every single time. Until the day I decided to heal the pattern.

I sat myself down as if I was having a client session with myself. No more hiding. What is the underlying pattern? What if I were ready to love myself enough no matter what? What if it was safe for me to see that pattern without shaming myself for it, denying or criticizing? What if instead I chose to forgive myself fully and completely for whatever discovery I were to make and to love myself into a new way of being. I literally whispered something like, *ok, Vica… whatever we find here, I got you. I love you. I forgive you. There's got to be a better way. Let's find it…*

It didn't take days or even hours. I was ready. The pattern became quickly apparent: **the only reason I was betrayed by different people at different times was because I first betrayed the still small voice, the Spirit, the knowing, given to me via my intuition.**

Looking into the mirror of my soul and seeing this truth was painful and liberating at the same time. At that very moment, I decided that I will follow my intuition with a simple prayer in my heart, *God, this is what I feel you are trying to communicate to me. I am going to follow through and act. If this is not aligned with the divine will for me in the best and highest way, please re-direct me.*

Rest assured I got re-directed plenty of times! Sometimes the fastest way for us to get on the right path is to hit a dead end to eliminate future doubt. Here is a quick example. Let's imagine that you and I are hiking in the forest and somehow lose our way. Which in my life with a poor sense of geographic direction is not that hard to imagine! We come to a place where the path splits in two, and we don't know which will lead us to the main road. We both have a prompting that we need to take the path to our right. Now we are walking on this path for a brief ten minutes just to see that it leads us to the dead end. While we are frustrated, we now also know that the path to the left is the "right" one. We backtrack and get on it. After two long hours of walking, we are finally at the main road.

Had we chosen the path to the left at first, would we have stayed on it… faithfully? Or, doubting the length of the hike, would we have turned back after an hour? Or… as often happens in life after one hour and fifty minutes, the short ten minutes from our desired outcome? Would we have given up just steps away from our goal?

This redirection came in the form of getting my instructor's license in ThetaHealing® technique. I got a very clear feeling that I had to get certified in as many classes as an instructor as possible, polishing my intuitive skills and healing abilities. I followed immediately registering for the first available class in Brazil. Brazil felt just a little off, but hey, I was following the prompting and gave God full veto rights in redirecting me!

I was not put off by the fact that the host of the training seminar was not responding to my many inquires as to the venue or accommodations. I literally received the information for both two days prior to my scheduled departure. I was excited to see Brazil for the first time because my sister-in-law is Brazilian, and her dad was going to show me Rio prior to the training.

My excitement did not wear off when I arrived at the airport and realized that I did not have my passport! On average I travelled internationally at least several times a year for over twenty years, having never forgotten my passport before. I had plenty of time and my dad was available to bring my passport to me just in time. Yet, to my momentary dismay, I quickly found out that despite of my previous inquiry, Brazil now required a VISA which I did not have. I had no other choice but to cancel my trip.

Ok, I got you... get my education ASAP... but not starting in Brazil... ask... tune in... The Brazilian host did not refund my hosting fee, but at least the ThetaHealing Institute used the same tuition fee to cover the beginning of my basic training a few short months later in Valencia, Spain.

I lovingly speak of Valencia as one of the miracles of my divine timing, a path that is created for each one of us individually and is co-created through us as we own our birthright of divine sparks of light, literal children of GOD, Great Overall Designer. **All the times we ignore our intuition, all the times we follow it into the dead end, all of them are preparing us for the moment of when we choose to follow this gift of the still small voice to fulfill our beautiful and sacred mission on this earth, to enter our divine timing. And it always happens just at the right time.**

Valencia opened the doors both to some of my most meaningful relationships and significant healings in my life for me and my loved ones. With every passing year I am amazed at the depth of the roots that have taken place during that serendipitous trip, blossoming into joyful and expanding opportunities. Following God's voice, the Spirit's prompting via my faculty of intuition has not been a convenient or easy path without failures. But it has been the most remarkable journey of discovery of life's daily unexpected miracles.

February 2018 was a fun month of intuition vs reason. I got a feeling that it was time to rent a studio space for my YU2SHINE business. But, having sold real estate in the past and preaching the importance of ownership vs rent, I was resisting the urge to rent and actively reasoning it away. I had a lot of other great arrangements for the seminars that I taught until all of them started falling through one after the other following the prompting to rent! First, one of my friends and students who owned the yoga studio doubled booked her own space for the very seminar she was attending! I immediately moved it to my country club, only to be told that the seminar room I was accustomed to using was under reconstruction! There we were, me and my class, sitting in the open space over the tennis courts, attempting to meditate!

Taking the group through an exercise of aligned manifesting, where you first seek to know the best scenario for you to experience and then manifest it into your life, I was guided to manifest, you guessed it, a rental space for my business. In my mind's eye I witnessed an arched window of my office to be, allowing for abundant light. I finished teaching on Tuesday. On Wednesday I saw a few places with my realtor and recognized the very window in one of them. By Friday I had a signed leased… and a year later I was teaching the same seminar now in my own space.

I eagerly shared the story of manifesting my beloved studio with my students, telling them of the power of the guided manifestation and inviting them to do the same exercise with me. I held my breath with anticipation, asking Creator, *What am I here to manifest today?* Clearly and undeniably, I received an answer, *a trip to Hawaii…*

Leaning into all the combined past failures of not following the still small voice of the Spirit, I acted immediately. I called my mom, *Mom, can you take a week off work?... to go to Maui?...*

Sensing and following the urgency of the trip, a short week later, my mom and I arrived in our Air B&B, with no expectations and fully open to have a great adventure. We were mesmerized by the views of waterfalls and serene, lush nature both from the helicopter and a winding road to Hana. We saw a whale do a full jump out of the water in front of us and enjoyed some excellent food between our many excursions. It was during one of the nights that I literally was awoken by a gentle voice, *grab a notebook...* I fervently started jotting down the inspired ideas I was receiving for many years to come for my business. A map was unfolded for me and through me, a journey that I have been on since that moment of divine clarity. I was given an idea for our company's first app... and the second... and... the creativity flood was open as was my heart to receive deeper guidance, requiring greater determination of action.

A few short months later in July 2019, we were going down to the beach for our annual family trip, when, the subtle feeling unmistakably occurred again, and I heard myself repeat it out loud while driving the car, *I think we are going to buy a beach house while on this trip!* Time seemed to both stand still and speed up at the same time. Within our one vacation week, we have identified and went under a contract for a beach home that we could only see for 15 minutes. The feeling was calm, peaceful, and clear, *this is the home.* My logical mind screamed leaning into my well-overused ability to reason, *but we cannot get qualified for the loan!* The Spirit via my intuition once again re-assured, *this is the home.*

Miracle upon miracle, from a sudden dip in the interest rate, making our purchase possible and satisfying the demands of logic and reason, to a hurricane passing by without harming our brand-new investment, I found myself overwhelmed with gratitude for the whole journey. I was witnessing **how uniquely loved we are by our Creator and how powerfully equipped we are to walk our path when we choose to follow the guidance of the still small voice.**

So, when in December of 2019 the feeling came to take all my seminars and create a Quantum Freedom group subscription online instead, I listened. Instead of reasoning against it, I harmonized my reason with my intuitive guidance that I could work from my beautiful beach home, where I was planning on spending the off season writing and creating. We launched the group in January 2020, a few short months prior to the island and the world shutting down for the COVID pandemic. I sat on my deck, watching the dolphins dance in the waves, and crying, both in deep sorrow for the fear that was suffocating so many, and in amazement that we were now working on My Grief set for our Empower-mE app to help others to process the engulfing energy of grief.

I had to release any shame of being safe when so many others were not, when the same whisper that has brought me to this place has redirected my purpose, *you are to create and bring more light through the darkness that is descending. Focus on the light.* I listened to the voice. I continued to create the programs while witnessing our online family growing and expanding, for some, leaning into the light of the group as their only support system.

I listened and followed the voice again and again, creating one season of the podcast *All About the Voice,* dedicated to expanding one's intuition. And in January 2021, a month prior to Russia invading my homeland Ukraine I was guided to add a Russian-speaking group to our subscription, which has since become a beacon of peace, light, hope, and comfort to many.

Before every session for our group, I ask for divine alignment and guidance. I lean into God-given gift of intuition, and I trust. I trust

God's LOVE for each of us. I trust peace and light to prevail. **I trust that if you are reading these words, this is your time to trust. Your divine timing is here. Ask, "*What am I to manifest now? What is my next step to take?*" Act and witness miracles unfold.**

VICTORIA RADER, PH.D. POSSIBILITY COACH

Victoria Rader, Ph.D. Possibility Coach™, transformational speaker, founder of YU2SHINE, internationally best-selling author of Prosper mE: the 35 Universal Laws to Make Money Work for You (and three other books), creator of Empower-mE and Master-mE apps, founder of Free mE EFT and Quantum Freedom.

Victoria empowers her clients to grow in all areas of their life through the proven formula of success so that they have more PEACE, PURPOSE, and PROSPERITY.

In 2009 during the recession, Victoria became a successful top 1% of real estate agents while homeschooling her kids. Victoria started training and seeing the limitations imposed by the subconscious mind. Later she received PhD in Metaphysics to understand better how we create our daily reality. Victoria also got certified in many energy healing modalities and traditional success coaching approaches and have founded Free mE EFT and Quantum Freedom techniques as a way to free one's mind.

In her practice Victoria witnessed physical healings for her clients, including a miraculous heart healing for her nephew, as well as practical powerful shifts in finances, career, and relationships.

Victoria loves teaching on the universal/ God's laws and their practical daily application for people of faith and spiritual seekers – bridging the gap of judgement through LOVE (Life-Originating Vibrant Emotion).

In 2022, Victoria received CREA GLOBAL AWARD by Brainz Magazine along with Brene Brown, Richard Branson and others in recognition of creative and innovation ideas, adaptability in business, and contribution to sustainability and mental health projects.

Connect with Victoria at https://yu2shine.com/.